To all the women who so courageously shared their stories with me, those who are included in the book and those who are not—may God bring them continued healing.

To the woman who called me, wept, and then fled by hanging up—may God find her and touch her with healing.

To the thousands of women who still live with pain, grief, and guilt—may God find and heal them, too.

K.K.W.

Contents

Contents

Preface

On the day I finished editing this book, a pastor confided that, in earlier years of his ministry, he once counseled a woman to get an abortion. And she did. As he spoke, his strong voice quavered. Although we were speaking by telephone, I sensed that perhaps tears had momentarily come to his eyes. I thought of the title chosen for this book: *When the Crying Stops.*

That incident was like an "Amen" to the fifteen stories graphically recounted in this book, a solemn reminder that the crying doesn't stop in a lifetime for many who have succumbed to abortion's siren song. It doesn't stop for the mother who cannot blot out the memory of assembly-line abortions in a crowded clinic. The crying doesn't stop when bitter-sweet reminders signal what that baby might have been. When it ends for the baby, it barely has begun for those who will miss that baby's cries.

Still, there is an end, a healing, for all who turn in faith to Christ. The crying will stop forever in his heaven. With Jesus then in glory, there will be no more tears. With him now in forgiveness, the tears become fewer and fewer.

Those who read this book will likely be inclined to shed a few tears in compassion. May you be touched by both the human pathos and the divine intervention.

Gary P. Baumler

A Note to Women Who Have Experienced or Are Considering Abortion

If you are a woman thinking of having an abortion or suffering from guilt and regret after one, we urge you to seek Christian counsel. Help is available. Talk with your minister. Through your church you can get information about Christian agencies and counselors, counseling hotlines, and support groups. If you have no other place to turn, you are encouraged to call WELS Lutherans for Life: 1-800-729-9535.

Look for the comfort and direction that God alone offers through his Scriptures.

I will praise the LORD, who counsels me; even at night my heart instructs me. I have set the LORD always before me. Because he is at my right hand, I will not be shaken. (Psalm 16:7,8)

Introduction

One and a half million women choose to have elective abortions every year in the United States, ending more than one in every four pregnancies. That's 4000 lives every day, one every 10 seconds. In just the 19 years since abortion on demand was legalized, more than 25 million abortions have been performed on at least 15 million women. (Approximately 40% of women having abortions are repeat cases.)

The enormity of that number is hard to fathom. A great deal has been written about those 25 million unborn babies. But, until recently, not much was known about the 15 million—the women who had the abortions.

Little reliable research has been done on postabortion women for several reasons. First, many, if not most, women who have had an abortion keep it a secret. A few are willing to speak out, but they are only a few. Most women hide it all their lives. Second, abortion clinics do little follow-up beyond giving the woman instructions on what to do in case of fever or bleeding. Some may call a few days later; many do not even do that. Certainly none call months or years later, when symptoms of distress characteristic of postabortion syndrome are most likely to occur. Third, the political climate in our country blocks such follow-up studies. To admit that abortion may cause significant problems is not "politically correct." The medical community doesn't admit it. Certainly those who work to keep abortion legal don't want to admit it.

Dr. Vincent M. Rue, Co-Director of the Institute for

Abortion Recovery and Research, says, "Of the several hundred studies done on abortion's psychological aftermath, all reveal some percentage of negative effects. The fact that most of these studies report few negative results stems from the reality that most of the studies polled women hours or days after the abortion. During this time frame, women commonly report feelings of relief. However, months or years later, the pain and suffering from the impacted grief can be triggered, and then women commonly describe feeling overwhelmed."

A few clinicians, however, here and in Europe, have truly listened to their patients and begun studying and documenting the existence of problems with the aftermath of abortion. Their studies have yielded differing results, reporting a rate of psychological complications that ranges from 10 to 50 percent. Using just twenty percent of those 15 million women who have had abortions means three million women have suffered distress after abortion since abortion was legalized. Remember, that's a conservative estimate.

Where are these women to go for help? The medical community is not helping them. The psychological community, largely, does not recognize their problems as legitimate. Church-based support and counseling groups are about the only ones helping, and they are far too few to cope with the flood of troubled women. Most women are left to deal with the aftermath of abortion alone.

Abortion's Aftermath

Abortion can cause an array of short and long term emotional problems. When a woman first realizes she is pregnant with a baby that she feels she doesn't want or can't handle, she is often frightened and desperate. Often the baby's father abandons her, and she may be afraid to tell anyone else. She needs to solve her problem quickly.

She may turn to abortion as a solution even though deep inside she may be going against her own moral beliefs. She may even truly wish to keep the baby but sees no way to provide for it. Women everywhere speak the same refrain: "I felt I had no other choice."

Going against your moral code or doing something that you really don't want to do is fraught with danger. Immediately after the abortion, the woman is likely to feel immense relief because her "problem" has been "solved." For many women, however those unresolved conflicts will come back later to haunt them.

It may be months later. It may be years later. The haunting may be triggered by the anniversary of the abortion or the date when the baby would have been born. It may be triggered when the woman has another child and realizes the baby she aborted was no different from the one she holds in her arms. It may be triggered when she loses a much-wanted later pregnancy or has trouble conceiving.

Whatever sets them off, such feelings can eventually engulf a woman. The abortion can never be undone; the woman has to find a way to cope with the pain. She may rationalize her choice by telling herself "it was only a blob of tissue." She may repress the memory—many women remember their actual abortion procedures only vaguely. Such defense mechanisms may work for a while, but eventually she may begin to experience further post-traumatic symptoms:

- **Guilt.** When a woman begins to admit that she killed her child, the guilt can overwhelm her. She may see herself as a worthless person. She may ask, "How could I have ever done such a thing?"
- **Anxiety.** A postabortion woman may suffer from extreme tension, physical symptoms (such as pounding heart or frequent headaches), difficulty concentrating, insomnia, or generalized worry.

- **Emotional numbness.** After an abortion, a woman may try to flatten her emotions, to avoid feeling anything too deeply. That can have severe consequences for future relationships.
- **Depression.** A few postabortion women reach the point of a true clinical depression. Others just live with constant, low-level sadness. Sudden crying episodes, lowered self-concept, lowered sexual response, buried anger, and disruption of relationships can all result.
- **Unusual psychological responses.** Some postabortion women become upset around the anniversary of the abortion, or the date when the baby would have been born. Others experience flashbacks to the abortion procedure, triggered by common events such as a gynecological exam or machinery that sounds like the abortion equipment. Some women suffer agonizing dreams about babies.
- **Anxiety over future childbearing or intense desire to become pregnant.** Some women, after an abortion, are terrified that they may never have another baby. They may need to prove to themselves that they can have another child, so they become pregnant as soon as possible. Some women have a baby they hope will replace the aborted child—placing an unfair burden on that baby. Others have repeated abortions, as if trying to prove that they can still conceive.
- **Self-punishing behavior.** Some women escape into alcohol or drug use to numb the pain. Others go through phases of sexual promiscuity or enter abusive relationships. Certainly, we cannot say that having an abortion is the only reason women do these self-destructive things,

but they occur in a disproportionately high percentage of women who have had abortions.

Hope for Healing

What must a woman do to heal? Time alone won't do it; neither will ignoring the pain and "getting on with your life," as well-meaning friends and counselors may advise. The postabortion woman has several steps she must work through.

Spiritually, the first two steps are preparation: repentance and grieving. Steps three and four are turning in faith to God for forgiveness and living as one who is forgiven.

- Step one: the woman must overcome denial and admit that it was her child she aborted. That sounds harsh, but healing can't come as long as she refuses to accept what really happened.
- Step two: she needs to grieve for that child. She probably hasn't done that, and society certainly hasn't encouraged her to grieve. But she has experienced a loss, and grieving is a necessary part of healing. It is a uniquely human and individual process that takes time.
- Step three: she needs to listen to God's message of forgiveness in Christ. She may know, she may have always known, that God forgives. But she needs to accept that forgiveness, to let go of "but God couldn't forgive this sin; it's too great." God forgives every sin. This one is no exception.
- Step four: she needs to forgive both herself and any others involved in the abortion. Holding on to anger at herself, the baby's father, or anyone else who encouraged her to have the abortion can only be destructive.

Only after these steps have been taken can a woman

finally begin the healing process. She shouldn't expect herself simply to forget the abortion, however, but to come to peace with it. As so many women have told me, "I finally feel free of the guilt, but the sadness will never go away."[1]

A Word about How This Book Was Written

This book is the result of in-depth interviews with 19 women who have had abortions, some more than one, and experienced problems afterward. For some it was a recent experience; for others it was many years ago. The women range in age from 22 to 63. Their backgrounds run the gamut from farm, to suburb, to inner city. Most are white; one is black. All of them have at least begun healing, but some are further along in the process than others.

The women were located in two ways. Some were found through postabortion counseling groups. Others responded to an ad placed in a Christian magazine asking for women to share their stories anonymously for this book.

All the women's names have been changed. Details about their geographic locations and identifying characteristics of their lives have also been changed.

Those women who live within driving distance I interviewed in person; those flung across the country I interviewed by telephone. All the interviews were taped. The interviews lasted an average of two hours, although some were much longer.

The interviews were emotional experiences in themselves. Some of the women had never told anyone else about their abortions. Others speak freely, even in public, about their experiences. We sat together, the women and I, either at their kitchen tables or at the telephone, in

---

[1] One excellent source of further information on the aftereffects of abortion is a booklet *Help for the Postabortion Woman* by Reisser and Reisser, published by Focus on the Family, Pomona, CA 91799 and available from Northwestern Publishing House.

pools of lamplight in sleeping houses. We shared laughter; we shared many, many tears; in some cases we shared hugs. Every one of those women touched my heart in a unique and special way. Their bravery was astounding. Their sense of caring for other women in the same position was inspiring. I thank them with all my heart.

I have used their words very much the way they were spoken. Of course, I have done some editing. People tend to speak in a much more wordy fashion than other people want to read, so I have done some condensing. For ease of reading, since many of the women's abortion experiences were so chaotic that they remember them in disjointed leaps and jumps, I have rearranged things into chronological order. On the whole, however, I have used the women's words.

Many of the women spoke of their belief that their babies are in heaven and that they will be reunited with them some day. While the Scriptures are silent on this issue, the women place their hope in our merciful and loving God.

One thing that's hard to reproduce on paper is the emotion with which words are spoken. Many times the women broke down crying and stopped speaking. Sometimes their words were so tear-choked they are hard to understand on the tape. I have indicated these "tear breaks" with a series of dots . . . .

I have written this book for two audiences. One is the pregnant woman who is considering an abortion. Women have not been given accurate information about abortion, fetal stages of development, or all of the options open to them. It's not in the interest of the abortion industry (which takes in millions of dollars a year) to give out complete information about the risks. Women need to know about all the possible complications, including the psychological and spiritual ones.

The other audience is the woman who has suffered the aftereffects of abortion and struggles alone with it. I particularly remember one woman who responded to the magazine ad by calling the publisher and asking for my phone number. Then, late one winter night, she called me. She was frightened; her voice shook and broke with tears. She said she had had an abortion but she didn't want to talk about it that night. She wanted to make an appointment for the next week. She would not tell me her first name or give me her phone number. She promised to call back on the appointed night and abruptly hung up. I never heard from her again.

Many other women like her are out there, women struggling alone with their guilt and grief. I hope this book will persuade them to seek help, either in a postabortion group, from a member of the clergy, with a Christian counseling service, or from a trusted friend. They need so much to hear the message of God's love and forgiveness.

I pray that message comes through as the women tell their stories.

Kathy Winkler

A Word about the Poems

When I was asked to try my hand at writing a devotion to go with each of the chapters in this remarkable book, I turned immediately to the Psalms. The Book of Psalms is the church's prayer book. Down through the ages men and women have found peace and solace in its penetrating depths and soaring heights.

I quickly discovered the task was much bigger than I. How do you speak the word of God into the dark void of death that is abortion's aftermath? Quite by accident, I found my words lapsing into free verse. It seemed to me the deep pain that spilled from each woman's story cried out for an answer deeper than mere prose. In these poems I've tried to tell each woman's story straight, but the gospel straighter still.

If you're struggling with the memory of abortion, I hope you find a road to healing on these pages—the healing Christ alone can give. He gives it in the company of his church. Seek out your pastor, or if you have none, find one soon in whom you can confide. The careful reader will discover my conviction that God's tools for healing are his word and sacrament.

Each free verse devotion begins by citing the woman's own words. A text from one of the Psalms provides a hinge toward healing. In most cases my poems are divided into two parts: first we hear the woman's pain, then Christ's healing voice.

For further prayer the reader is encouraged to turn to

the entire Psalm from which the text comes. Pray that Psalm aloud. The Psalms teach us to pray not from the poverty and weakness of our sinful heart but from the richness and depth of God's own word. While you pray, remember Jesus Christ prays with you. *It is the incarnate Son of God, who has borne every human weakness in his own flesh, who here [in the Psalms] pours out the heart of all humanity before God and who stands in our place and prays for us.*[2]

Over the years I've been privileged to minister personally to some who've faced abortion's aftermath. These poems are dedicated to those courageous people to whom I've spoken Christ's consoling word of forgiveness and healing face to face: both women who were mothers of aborted babies and men who were their fathers.

If you, O LORD, *kept a record of sins, O Lord, who could stand? But with you there is forgiveness; therefore you are feared.* (Psalm 130:3,4)

Harold L. Senkbeil

---

[2] Dietrich Bonhoeffer, Psalms: the Prayer Book of the Bible, Minneapolis: Augsburg Publishing House, 1970. pp. 20f.

Judy

Judy is the "California Girl," straight out of the song. Attractive, athletic, free-spirited, she jumped into life with zest. Unfortunately, in her rush to try everything life held, she also jumped into drugs.

Like so many children of the seventies, drugs gripped her like a vise, draining away her love of life.

Drugs cost Judy a lot: her self-esteem, her athlete's body, for a while her child, and the two babies she aborted.

But God turned Judy's life around. Today she says she's the mother of eight children—but she only has six of them. The other two she's still missing, and she's still dealing with her guilt.

Like so many women in the pro-life movement, Judy is there because she knows the reality of abortion. She's been there and left two children behind.

† † † † †

I grew up in California. I was adopted at six months and have no idea who my birth mother is. I had a happy childhood as far as I can remember, until I was in high school, that is. After I turned 15 or 16, I wasn't too happy.

My dad was domineering—very domineering. If he loved us, (I have a brother three years younger than me) that's how he showed it. I still don't honestly know if he really loved us.

1

Then there's my mom; I don't know how to describe my mom. She really didn't show much love either. She was very reserved, but somehow I knew she loved me.

There was no religion in our house. My mother was a Christian until she married my dad, but he wasn't. I went to Sunday school until I was four. Then, my mother tells me, something happened, and I wouldn't go back. She doesn't know what it was, and I don't remember.

There was a lot of fighting in our house, fighting over everything. My father is very opinionated. He's right and everyone else is wrong. I was afraid of him, very meek. He never hit us. He never spanked us or did anything. He didn't have to. All he had to do was raise his voice, and I cowered. Up until I was about 16, I did everything he said; but after I turned 16, I started to rebel.

I was very involved in sports in high school, so I wasn't home a lot. I wouldn't get home until after 6:00. I'd do my homework and go to bed, so I didn't have a lot of contact with my parents. I never had a date in high school; I was still a tomboy. I didn't want to have anything to do with boys except to play sports with them—and I liked that because I was better than the other girls!

Then I discovered drugs. It wasn't offered to me by the man standing on the corner as is the popular notion. I had to look for it. I took my first drink of beer when I was about 15, and I loved it. I loved it right from the beginning. I figured if beer was good, then drugs were going to be better, so I went looking. I started asking a few questions, and it didn't take long to find. I didn't like pot, so I used mostly LSD. I never had a bad trip; I liked it right from the start. It was an escape for me—maybe I was bored, bored with sports, bored with school—I don't really know. School was always very easy for me. I could get B's without studying, A's if I studied.

I was able to continue with sports even though I was

using drugs. I did them mostly when I didn't have practice or a game. I tried almost anything I could get my hands on. Besides LSD, I also liked barbiturates, when I could get them, but they weren't as easy to find. I didn't drink much hard liquor during high school, just the drugs.

After graduation I stayed at home, kept doing drugs, and tried to go to school; but that wasn't very appealing to me. My parents found out about the drugs, and, obviously, they weren't happy with me. My father came down on me at various times, but that was nothing new. They took me to a counselor, but I wasn't ready to stop then.

I'd go to school for a while and then drop out, complete some more classes and then drop out again. Finally, I got a job at a record store. The store and the drugs fit together hand-in-hand for me. I could get high at work and still do OK, and everything would be all right.

I lived at home off and on, moving into apartments and then back home when I ran out of money. I wasn't making that much, and most of my money went to buy drugs.

When I used drugs, I wasn't as shy and was more outgoing. That's probably why I used them. I was more friendly (I thought) and wasn't as afraid to be around people. At that point I would say I was psychologically addicted to the drugs, perhaps not physically addicted, but certainly addicted to the environment that drug use creates.

I was very attractive. Because I was so athletic, I had a very good figure. Cheerleaders were jealous of my figure. Of course, I took it for granted. I looked like the typical athlete: short brown hair, green eyes, and freckles. I attracted my share of male attention—more than my share.

During that period, when I was 19, I became sexually active. My first experience was with one of my bosses. Until I was 17, I literally didn't know what sex was. No one ever told me, and I really couldn't figure out what people

3

did—what went where. When I found out, I was scared to death—appalled and scared. It almost made me sick. I knew that unless I was high I wouldn't be able to do it. But I was curious, so I took some barbiturates and I did it. I didn't find it pleasant; I was disgusted.

It was the first time I'd ever had sex, and I got pregnant. Everyone who knew said an abortion was the perfect thing for me to do. At that point in my life, I always did the opposite of what people told me to do, so I didn't get an abortion, even though my dad had made an appointment for me. I knew several girls who had babies and were living on welfare. They were on their own, had money coming in, and, at the time, that was appealing to me—to get away from my family and be on my own and have an income. I had no concept of what a baby was.

I went to a home for unwed mothers, had my baby (a girl), and I kept her. Right after I had her, my parents bought me a small house. I paid rent to them, and they were the perfect grandparents. I got along better with them for a while.

When I saw my baby I thought, "So this is love." I don't think I'd ever felt love before; it was a whole new experience for me. I had stopped taking drugs while I was pregnant and didn't go back on them for three years. I mostly stayed home, collected welfare, and took care of my daughter. I think I was a good mother at first.

I liked it so much that by the time she was a year old I was pregnant again. This one was from a closer relationship than the first one, but when I got pregnant, I found out he was married. I never told him about the pregnancy, and I had an abortion.

People had started telling me, neighbors and friends, that there was no way I could handle two kids by myself (although I knew I could). I was enrolled at the state college at that time. People kept telling me to stay in school, and in a few years I'd have my degree, and everything would be perfect. They said my daughter would be able to have this and that, and I'd meet a man and get married.

My daughter's pediatrician told me that what I had in my uterus was only a few cells capable of becoming a human being. That was all I needed to hear. I thought it was true. It didn't even dawn on me that there was a real, live baby there. I don't even know why, this time, I did what everyone told me to do. Making the decision was very traumatic for me. I bought maternity clothes; I took them back. I bought them again; I took them back again. All through this, not once did anybody say to me, "Keep it." Not one person. For the first time in his life my dad didn't butt in—I wish he had.

I knew about adoption. After all, I'm adopted. I knew also that, if I carried the baby, I wouldn't give it up for adoption. I really didn't want an abortion. All I needed was for one person to say "Don't" and I wouldn't have. But no one did.

I changed my mind so many times that, by the time I decided, I was more than four months along, so I had to have a saline abortion.

I remember sitting in the lobby crying before they did it. One of the counselors came up to me and said that after I had my abortion everything would be all right and that she'd take me shopping. It sounded like this was something everyone did, every day.

So they did it, and nothing happened. I stayed in the hospital for three days, waiting for this "cell" to be aborted. Still nothing happened. So I went home. I remember thinking, "I'm glad it didn't work." I kept wondering why I had ever gone through with it in the first place.

A week later I was up at college, and my water broke. The baby came out, but the umbilical cord didn't. I drove myself 45 minutes up the highway to get to a hospital, with the baby next to me on the seat. I finally had to pull off the freeway because I was getting so faint. I pulled into a gas station and told the guy that I was having a miscarriage. He called the paramedics, and they took me the rest of the way. I didn't look at the baby. Maybe if I had, it would have been even worse. I remember that the nurses were so mad at me they were slamming instruments around. I think it was just frustration on their parts. They saw that helpless little baby, I didn't. I put myself in their shoes. How many women want to have a baby and can't?

I wasn't the same afterwards. I felt different. I don't know exactly how, but different. All my feelings were gone. I was numb, just going through the motions. I didn't seem to have any feelings about the abortion at all.

I remember I tried to get pregnant a couple of times, but I didn't. Most of the men were acquaintances or friends, basically one-night-stands.

I also gained a lot of weight. Then a friend told me that she had lost weight using angel dust (PCP, a veterinary tranquilizer used on horses), so I started using it to lose weight too. It worked, but I almost lost my mind with it. I used it for about eight months, and then I just fell apart— literally. My weight dropped from 140 to just under 100 pounds. At my height and muscular build, I looked like I was dead. I had doctors giving me prescriptions for peanut butter and jelly sandwiches to gain weight!

I got real sloppy. I got arrested twice for drug use. The second time the county decided I was an unfit mother, and they took my daughter away from me. I wasn't neglecting her, but I have to admit I wasn't a fit mother. I was high around her all the time. I got pregnant again, and that was my second abortion. I was deathly afraid of what the PCP had done to my baby (I would have dreams at night about a deformed baby), so I did it. I smoked some PCP just before going in for the abortion. The

thought had crossed my mind that, if I smoked before I
went in, maybe I wouldn't wake up. They put me under,
and I stopped breathing; but they gave me oxygen, and I
woke up. I was home in four hours.

I had totally lost control. I didn't know who God was at
that time, and I had no idea that he was in control. I wasn't
even me; I was somebody else. When I think about that
period of my life, it's like me watching someone else.

After they took my daughter, I somehow managed to
get myself into a drug rehab center. By that time I wanted
to stop using drugs; I was so tired and couldn't go on any
more. I was in for 30 days, and when I got out I had gotten
some strength back and gained some weight. I got a good
job and stayed at it for 18 months. I stayed clean and got
my daughter back.

Then I got pregnant again, but I was determined to
keep this one. There was no question; there weren't going
to be any more abortions. There wasn't anything emotional about it. It just was. I had a boy. The first six months
were rough. He cried a lot, and I had postpartum depression, but after that things got better. I stayed relatively
clean. I'd occasionally have a drink, but I didn't do any
drugs. I completed EMT training and was looking for a
job.

My daughter was ready for kindergarten, and I put her
in a Christian school. I don't know why I chose that
school. I can only say it was the Holy Spirit. I didn't have
any idea who God was, who Jesus was, at that time. I had
no concept of anything, but the idea was appealing to me,
so I put her in the school. Her teacher kind of took me
under her wing, and that's how I found out about the
Lord. I thought I had become a Christian. I sort of played
around with it—I was and then I wasn't. It didn't really
touch me.

Then I found out I was pregnant again. I seriously considered another abortion, but I couldn't find anyone who was doing them at that time. I remember after calling around, just sitting there thinking, "Well, I don't want this abortion anyway." So I had another baby, another girl.

I decided at that point that I wasn't going to have any more relationships until I found one that I would be married into. I lived in an apartment with my three kids, on welfare, and we were doing fine. Then I met a man and became pregnant again. I never used any birth control. I'm sure it was because I wanted to be pregnant. I can't explain it, but I had this need to be pregnant. It was so strong that nothing could have stood in the way. I figured, if I couldn't have love, I'd have my kids. I loved them, and, even if the man didn't love me, I'd have them. I think I was a good mother. I was always there with my kids. I never had men in the apartment with my kids, or drug users. I sheltered them from all of that. They lived a relatively normal life. They just didn't even know about it all.

The father of my fourth child was a man I really liked. He was single, clean-cut, quiet, and well-mannered, and a Christian. I wanted a relationship with him. We ended up getting married before the baby was born.

My husband became very active in church. He really believed, and he'd want me to go to church with him. You see, I'm a person who always has to understand everything. I could never understand how someone could die and be raised from the dead and go somewhere that I've never seen. So I always said, "I'm not wasting my time on that," and he'd reply, "OK, I'll pray for you."

I had enrolled my kids in his church's school. The pastor kept coming over, and I'd sound off to him, going back and forth. But he kept coming back and coming back. The two of them, my husband and the pastor, didn't really hound me, but it was always there. The seed was planted.

Suddenly one day it seemed that I just understood that

you don't understand it; you just believe it. I started going to church with him.

The guilt over my abortions started when I became a Christian and I realized what I had done. Before that I hadn't really realized it. I hadn't told anyone except my husband about it. I was dealing with it by thinking about it and reading books.

I know that, as much as I hate myself for what I did, God has forgiven me, and that's helped the most. It's probably why I am so committed to trying to stop other people. I've already been forgiven, and, even though I still have a hard time with it, I want to channel that energy to somebody else. I want to stop someone else so they don't have to go through the same thing I did.

I still cry about it, and it still bothers me; but I think I'm healed enough that I can say, "OK, this happened; but I'm forgiven, and I need to start helping some other people." If I can get my message to others, I'll feel more healed.

I haven't really started yet because it's just become important to me, and I don't know where to start. I feel it needs to be done on an individual level. I need to walk up to one person at a time and say, "Don't do it," like I wish someone had to me. I want so badly to get my message to other women, but I just don't know yet how to go about it.

I am so definitely pro-life. There's no two ways about it. We need to stop abortion. I was born in 1956. If there had been abortion then, I wouldn't be here. I feel so strongly about this in my heart that I'm sure it's the reason I'm here.

I'd love to be a counselor at a crisis pregnancy center, if I can find one. I think about all those women out there. I don't know if the word is naive, but they just don't know. I don't know how many other women, if someone just said, "No, don't do it," would walk away.

I'm not the kind of person who walks a picket line or

lies down on a sidewalk. That's not where my interest is. My interest is in getting to the women, because they are the ones who are walking into the abortion clinics.

I'd also like to work with postabortion women. Even though my postabortion problems were delayed so many years, I can still feel all those feelings. My first abortion was 13 years ago and it still hurts to talk about it. It's like losing a child. I did lose those children; I killed them. Time has a way of healing things, but not this. This is not ever going to heal completely. It's like being an alcoholic. You are a recovering alcoholic, not recovered. I will never be a recovered postabortion woman, but I am recovering.

My husband and I have had three more children since our marriage, so now I have six. I'm a stay-at-home mother and am very content. You know, for some reason I've always wanted eight children, and I do have eight.

But I'm missing two.

JUDY: *I'm missing two*

**As the deer pants for streams of water,
so my soul pants for you, O God.** (Psalm 42:1)

*the emptiness is real
there's a hole inside
too big to fill
with all the stuff of life*

*and it hurts
the memories are pain
it hurts so much*

*how fill that hole?
how heal that pain?
how ease that loss?*

*I should have eight
but
two are gone
their toddler steps
their childhood pranks
their teenage jokes
will never be*

*I'm missing two
I took their lives away
now
two are gone
I have six
but
I'm missing two*

*quiet, child
I cannot bring your children back
but
I can give you love
and comfort you
I'll dry your tears*

*and
ease your pain
and
fill that hole*

*I've paid the price, you see
the awful price of sin
all the sins of all the world
and
your sin, too:
the loss of two
whose lives you took
that ugly sin and pain
I took on me*

*now here's life
and hope
and joy*

*in me you're whole
and strong
complete
you're missing two
I miss them too
but I forgive you
and
I love you
my love is bigger
than your pain*

*having me
you're missing none*

*so hush now, child
be strong
and whole
in me*

Mikki

Mikki is still not dealing with the aftereffects of her abortion. She admits it. When it bothers her, she just turns it off. Does something else. Doesn't think about it.

Mikki grew up in an alcoholic home, and she learned early and well the first rule of the child of an alcoholic: Don't talk about it. Don't admit it's there. Some therapists call it the "elephant in the living room" syndrome. There's an elephant in the living room, but nobody acknowledges its presence. Nobody talks about it.

There's certainly something in Mikki's room—the child she aborted over ten years ago. Her voice fills with tears and breaks as she talks, yet in the next sentence she says it doesn't bother her because she doesn't think about it. She says she knows that she is forgiven, but in the next sentence says that she doesn't know how she could be.

Only two people know about Mikki's abortion: a college roommate she rarely sees and her husband. He doesn't see the elephant in the living room either.

Perhaps, Mikki says, doing this interview will push her along the road to dealing with her feelings. Then again, maybe it won't.

††††

I grew up on the East Coast, near Boston. I lived in a white, middle-class, small town. Kind of boring. My father was an alcoholic. He's dead now, been dead for a couple of years. I would say, in looking back, that, although my life seemed normal to me at the time, because that's what I grew up with, it really was not.

I never had a good relationship with my father; none of us did. I have two brothers and a sister. I'm the youngest. He wasn't violent when he drank; he just kind of went off into his own little world. He almost became like a child—if he didn't get his way, he would sulk or have a tantrum. I wasn't afraid of him; I learned to stand up to him at a very early age. I didn't take a lot of his garbage. I just stood right up to him and never backed down. That was my defense, my way of coping with it.

I remember feeling as a kid that my mother was like my savior. She'd try to intervene, to keep things as peaceful as possible. Looking back I don't think that her staying in that situation and keeping us in it was a good thing; but she did what she felt she needed to do, and it's not for me to blame her. I felt close to her at the time. I definitely felt that she loved me, although I was never sure about my father. My mother used to say that he did, but he just wasn't the type to say it. It would have been nice to hear it once or twice.

We never talked about sex. I remember once asking my mother, "Mom, when are you going to talk to me about sex?" She said, "I'll talk to you when my mother talks to me." I thought that, after four kids, it was probably a little late for her! I suppose I could have gone to her if I'd wanted to, but I just didn't.

In high school I never did apply myself. I was one of those who was just happy to get by. I dated some, but not a lot. Still, I became sexually active quite early, when I was only 16.

I went to college and graduated with a degree in elementary education. I guess you would say I was a touch promiscuous in college and after. After I graduated, I moved to a big city in Texas and dated a lot of people. I met a guy and got pregnant. It was a big surprise—obviously nothing I'd planned. It just happened. Bingo.

That may sound callous, but that's how it was. I was single, living with some friends, had a good job, and was having a good time. Having a baby just wasn't in the cards. I told the father, and he said he had no intention of marrying me. He made his intentions quite clear right from the get-go. I had no desire to marry him either. I didn't think a child was the right reason to get married. He said he'd pay for an abortion.

Adoption was, quite truthfully, not an option I ever considered, and I don't know quite why. It was like my options were to get married and have this kid or have an abortion, and there was no third option. I couldn't tell you the reason.

At the time I thought that I could never give a child up, but now I look back and wonder how I could have done what I did. Giving it up would have been so much better. I didn't really think of this as being a little person. It was a purely selfish decision. All I thought was, "What am I going to do now? This is a problem, and I have to take care of it."

I went to the doctor, and he suggested a clinic. It all happened so quickly. Looking back, I didn't agonize. I had to make a decision; something had to be done.

I did cry. I sat in the clinic and just bawled before I went in. I remember sitting in a big room with six or eight girls—some of them were very young, high school age—and someone was explaining the procedure. I started bawling, and the person who was explaining said that this is the point where most women cry; so I just went on with it.

I don't remember much about the abortion itself. I think I've blocked most of it out. The father dropped me off and picked me up after, but he didn't go in. I don't remember that there was much pain. I know I was upset, because I remember the doctor telling me I had to relax. It was over in no time. They had me lie down on a bed somewhere, and then I called for a ride home. I stayed off work for a couple of days. I didn't tell anyone except my roommate, who was an old college friend.

I stayed in Texas for another year and a half, and then I met my husband. While we were dating, I told him about the abortion. I told him that, if it was going to make a difference, I wanted it to happen then, not after we were married. He really didn't say anything; we've never talked about it. We got married and moved to the Midwest.

At the time of the abortion, it was a relief—"well, this is taken care of." I didn't think about it for quite a while—for years. When it really started bothering me was after my son was born, and he's now almost five. I couldn't believe how crazy I was about this kid, and how much they change things for you. I would look at him and think, "So this is the end result. Here's this little person. Did I make the right decision five years ago?" Of course it was too late to change things, but I would think, "Was it a boy? Was it a girl? If I hadn't done it, where would I be with that person now?" Until I had the end results of a pregnancy in my arms, I just hadn't thought about it.

I didn't know who to talk to or what to say, so I would just mull it over in my mind—try to come to terms with it by myself.

Possibly the reason I didn't get very emotional was because all my life I've stuffed things down. I've always had a little wall around me. This is an amateur analysis, but when something starts to trouble me, I'm real good at just pushing it away. I know I'm doing it, but I've never been one to break down over something. If it's bothering me, I just don't think about it. I've gotten real good at turning things off.

After I'd been married for several years, I started going to my husband's church. Up to that time, I was one who went to church on Christmas Eve, and that was about it. I would have said I was a Christian, but I don't think I was. I just never really thought about it. I pooh-poohed a lot of things. I went through membership classes at my husband's church, but it took a long time before I was ready to say that this is what I believe.

I never told the minister about the abortion. I've never told my mother or anyone else besides that friend and my husband. I didn't think it was anybody else's business.

Looking back, it's like it was a whole different life back then. The way I felt about myself, the lifestyle I was leading, was so completely different from now. I don't think I cared about myself very much. We partied a lot, were out in bars drinking, things that I would never do now, foolish things to do. I think now, "You were crazy. Someone was looking out for you because you shouldn't be here." I think that's true—when I think of the times I drove home after having more than one too many. . . .

But I'm here, and I have two wonderful children, so something was meant to be. I don't quite know what. I'm all settled down and usually asleep on the couch five minutes after the dishes are done! It's just a whole different life.

I'm not sure if what I feel now is guilt. It's more sadness that I did this and shouldn't have. I made a bad decision ten years ago. Regret, maybe.

Right now I can't say I have a sense of being forgiven by God. Maybe it's that I haven't forgiven myself. On Sunday when the minister says that it doesn't matter what you've done, it doesn't matter how bad it is, somehow in the back of my mind I think, "But this is *bad*, this is really, really bad." Somehow I haven't gotten past that yet. It's like intellectually you know something, but emotionally you're not sure. That's where I'm at: on one hand I know it, but on the other hand, I don't know.

I think about that child . . . and I wonder about it. . . . "Where is it now?" I feel it's in heaven; but then I think, "Will I meet up with that child? Then what's going to happen?" It doesn't make any sense, but I don't know what the answer is.

So I don't think about it. I go and do something else and just don't think about it. I've never told my husband how I feel. I don't know what he thinks about it, because we've never talked about it.

I know I have the typical adult-child-of-an-alcoholic pattern of not talking about things. I know all that, but I just. . . .

I suppose I'll have a major crisis one of these days. I'll just lose it, and then I'll do something about it.

But maybe not.

MIKKI: *Maybe it's that I haven't forgiven myself*

**When I kept silent, my bones wasted away
through my groaning all day long. (Psalm 32:3)**

don't talk
sure, it hurts
but whatever you do
just don't talk

don't let on
of course it's ugly
but whatever you do
just don't let on you know
then maybe
it won't hurt so much

don't say it
you can see the mess
you can feel the pain
just don't say it
then maybe
it'll go away

don't talk
don't let on
don't say it
this is how I learned
to handle pain
and guilt as well
the sin of others
and my own

silence
was supposed to make it go away:
all the hurt
and all the ugly things
that people said or did

silence
would vanish pain
but it never did

and so I learned
to carry
all my hurts:
the evils done to me
the evil I had done

all this I carried with me
a large and heavy load
of sin
and grief

a conspiracy, that's what it was
a conspiracy of silence
but silence
is not the answer

silence
never covers sin
silence
never eases pain
it's all still there
deep down within
what was done to me
and
what I've done as well
an ugly heavy load

now come, my child
and speak to me
come spill your hurt
come say your sin
your secret sin
your sin of ugly shame

silence
never covers sin
silence
never hides the shame
but my love will

I've sent my Son
to be your shame
I've given him
to bear your sin
your ugly secret sin

he bore all your grief
he carried all your anguish
all the sorrow
you can't bear to speak
he knows them all full well

he bore them all
on that cross of his
he wiped them all away
in that death of his

so come my child
and speak to me
come break the silence
come say your ugly secret sin
come tell your painful private grief

come
hide no more
there's now no shame
in sins confessed
to me or my own servant
his ear is mine
to hear your sin
his mouth is mine
to speak for me

he'll speak my word
to erase your sin
and wipe out your guilt
to ease your pain

and open up your life
to peace and joy and hope
my peace
my joy
my hope
for you
now come

19

Alexis

Alexis is a slender black woman with reddish hair and a fiery temperament to match. Though her parents were from the South, she was born and grew up in a northern, industrial city—a city that has one of the highest rates of teen pregnancy in the country. Her fiercely independent spirit showed up even in childhood, when she bucked against her mother's strong discipline.

She fell into the trap of early sexual activity, along with so many of her contemporaries, resulting in a pregnancy while she was still in high school. Because of her strong family support, she was able to finish high school and avoid the cycle of poverty that is the fate of so many teen mothers. Another child and marriage followed, and she seemed to have broken free of the stereotype; but a third unplanned pregnancy and an abortion rocked her world.

Alexis has turned her grief for the baby she aborted into a gritty, sidewalk-style activism. The founder of a local chapter of Blacks for Life, she isn't content just to sit and talk about her opposition to abortion. She works the sidewalks, picketing and trying to persuade women on the way into clinics to reconsider.

Her style isn't for everyone; some people will be uncomfortable with her tactics. But for her the ember of grief has erupted into a flame of activism.

† † † † †

My mother and father were both married twice. My

father's first wife died, and my mother was divorced. My mother and her first husband had four children, and with my father she had four more. We are all very close, like one big family. My parents are originally from the South, New Orleans, but I was born and raised in the North.

I think I had a pretty normal childhood. I can say that I was close to my parents, but my main memory of my mother is of her constantly disciplining us. And I didn't want that. Compared to most of the other parents in my neighborhood, she was strict. Now that I'm a mother and raising my own kids, I realize she wasn't all that strict! But I thought she was. As an adult, I got much closer to her.

Sex was definitely undiscussed in our house. As far as my mother was concerned, you had no reason to even think about sex. That was taboo. Therefore, what we learned, we learned from our girlfriends. I remember when I was about 10 asking my older, married sister where babies came from. She told my mother what I had asked, and my mother got very angry with me and wanted to know why I wanted to know! I was just curious of course, because I had no idea how people had babies.

Even after I got older, it still wasn't discussed. My mother's way of keeping us in line was to lie to us: if you kiss a boy you'll get pregnant; if he touches your breasts you'll get pregnant. She figured if she scared us enough we wouldn't want to talk about it or do it. But it didn't work. During high school, when I met the man who is now my husband, I found out those things weren't true.

We had sex before marriage, and I had my first child, a little girl, when I was 16. She still doesn't know that her father and I weren't married when she was conceived. I wasn't using any birth control. I knew about it, but I didn't know about it in the sense of it being available to me. Most kids today know where they can go to get birth control pills, but I didn't. And I sure didn't dare ask my mother about it!

I knew having sex before marriage was wrong. I believed in God, but I just put it aside because I felt that, since I was in love with this person and I was going to marry him, how could it be that wrong? I thought God would understand.

I went to a parochial school, and I know I learned about the Commandments and sin; but it was never applied to our daily lives. No one ever said that, even though this is a natural desire, you need to use some type of self-control. No one ever talked about it in those terms. I just heard, "Keep your dress down; keep your legs closed"—that was the only education. I knew other kids were doing it, so I didn't feel guilty. It was the natural thing for a teenager to do—just don't get caught—but God and religion weren't part of it. Still, I do remember that every time we had sex I would get down on my knees and pray to God that I wouldn't get pregnant. I always felt that God came through for me.

I also thought that another reason I was OK as far as God was concerned was because I wasn't sleeping with different boys. We put a stigma on girls who slept around—called them a slut. But that wasn't my case. This was the boy I planned on marrying.

I was terrified when I found out I was pregnant. I didn't know about all the things that would happen to me, like morning sickness. I thought you just missed your monthly, and that was all. I was going on my second month and was kind of scared, but I wasn't too sure what was happening. I remember telling my boyfriend that every morning when I smelled bacon cooking I felt like throwing up. My girlfriend had a book about pregnancy, and from that we figured out what was happening. I didn't know what to do. I knew my mother was not the type who would take this sitting down!

When I finally told her, she was depressed, upset, and mad, and disappointed in me, because I was her youngest girl and kind of her pride and joy. She always talked about what a great job Alexis does, in helping her clean and doing homework—that type of thing. So, when this happened, it was kind of like me throwing mud in her face. Of course, she was thrilled with her grandchild after I had the baby. I brought her home and kept going to school while my mother took care of her.

After graduation I started working, and my boyfriend and I lived together. I knew my parents wouldn't approve of that, so I lied and told them we were married. I figured I had put enough on them to deal with.

Then I turned around and got pregnant again. It was a shock to me—I didn't know you could get pregnant that soon, without even having your period. I had my second child, a boy, eleven months after the first.

It was a lot of responsibility, but I wasn't the type of person who believed in partying. I took care of my responsibilities. These were my children, my responsibility, and it wasn't as difficult as I thought it would be. If I were the type of teenager who just wanted to go out and have fun and got tired of being a mother, it would have been a lot harder. Not all girls are like that, but I was willing to handle it.

After my son was born I continued working, and everything was going OK. But a year later I missed my monthly again, and after you have a baby, you know when you are pregnant. I was like, "I don't believe this! How is this possible again?" I thought I was too young to have that many kids. I was only 18, and I still wasn't married. I worried about what people would think, what my mother would think. My boyfriend was upset, and that made it even worse. I started thinking about having an abortion.

Abortion wasn't talked about in our family, but I knew it

was wrong. Still, I didn't have anyone to *tell* me it was wrong. The doctors said it was legal and OK. I remember telling my girlfriend that I had to take care of this before I was three months along when it would become a baby.

I remember the day I had the abortion as if it were yesterday. I went to the clinic. The counselor took three of us into a room and asked us to tell why we wanted an abortion. When you listen to others who want to have an abortion, you can convince yourself that you are doing the right thing. We justified it real good. I don't remember their reasons, but mine was, "I already have two kids, and I can't afford it." They all agreed with me, "You're right, you can't afford it."

They called my name. I was nervous and scared, but I wanted to hurry up and have it over with. The worst thing about it was that, when it was over, they took the baby away in a mason jar. It had a piece of paper wrapped around it with a rubber band so you couldn't see it. I remember I was crying. Something in my conscience told me that was a baby—no matter how much I tried to explain it away or justify it—I knew in my heart that was a baby. I looked at the jar and I remember thinking, "If that wasn't a baby, then why are they hiding it?"

But there was nothing I could do at that point. I couldn't say, "Put it back in; I'm sorry I did this." I was crying, and there was no one there to comfort me. I knew my boyfriend—he was outside waiting on me—would hug me and tell me that everything was OK, but it really wasn't.

Right after, I was most concerned about getting back to normal physically. The remorse I felt in the clinic room went away and was replaced by relief. I got back into the swing of things and didn't think much about it. My boyfriend and I never talked about it. It was just pushed aside and we never spoke of it again. No one in my family ever found out.

Then, just a few months later, my mother died. That was a setback for me. No one in my family, close to me, had ever died before. I had never had to deal with that pain and hurt. She died very suddenly. We had just come back from out-of-town, and I remember she called and asked me to bring the kids over to see her. Later on, the telephone rang. I was sure it was her again. Then my boyfriend came and told me she'd had a heart attack and was dead. When it happens to you, you're never ready for it.

At that time I knew God, but I didn't have a personal relationship with him. I was very angry at him for taking my mother. It didn't make sense to me—she was only 54, and she was in good spirits and feeling good. I withdrew from God. My father wanted me to read a passage in the Bible before her funeral, and I just glanced at it to satisfy him. I didn't want to read anything from God when he had just taken my mother away.

It took me a long time to deal with her death. I missed her calls every day. I kept wishing I could say, "That's my mother on the phone," but I couldn't say that anymore.

About six months after she died, my boyfriend and I got married. We just went to the courthouse and did it privately. Nothing changed; it was just that now it was legal.

It was about that time, in the late 70's, when the debate about abortion really started. I remember some friends of mine talking about it, and I remember saying, "It depends on the person. If that's what they want, who can say if it's right or wrong?" Because I'd had one, I definitely wanted to justify it. But little things were starting to hit at me, even though I wasn't aware of it.

I had a couple of girlfriends at work who suddenly came to know the Lord. They changed so much—they were busy partying all the time, and suddenly they changed. It was like, "What happened to her?" There was one woman in particular who had had a horrible childhood. She was molested by her father and was a prostitute for a while; but now she was a child of God, and she had this joy about her. By seeing her, it made me even more curious. It made me examine myself, ask myself if I really was a Christian.

I remember going home and reading the Bible. I remember praying to God to show me what needed to be changed in my life and help me to change it. I wanted to be different and to live for him. It happened slowly; it's not something that happens all at once. I slowly began to have a love for God that I never had before. I realized I hadn't been much of a Christian before, even though I had considered myself a Christian all my life and was always a member of a church. Now I was growing as a Christian, with Christ living in me.

That's when the guilt of the abortion really hit me. It was hard. I remember being at work and hearing about abortion on a Christian radio station. I didn't know they were aborting babies as late as they were. Suddenly I thought, "Hey, you had your baby killed. No two ways about it. Now what are you going to do about it?"

I started getting involved in an abortion issues group, planning on speaking out against it, and that's when the pain really hit. So many nights I found myself on the bedroom floor, crying. Excuse me . . . .

You cry out and you wonder how you can . . . make amends . . . change things. "What can I do, God, what?" And you realize that you can't, it's like there's no answer there. I thought, "I can deal with my mother's death, God, because you took her. But when it comes to my child . . . I did." I tried to tell myself that I didn't know at the time, but I did. After I had the abortion, I looked at the jar, and I knew that was a baby.

I thought maybe I'd do some work with women who were considering having an abortion, so I went to a training session for counselors for a local crisis pregnancy center. The trainer was talking about the symptoms that women who have had an abortion suffer from, and everything she said was like, "How does she know that about me?" Everything she said was me. Later she went around the group and asked everyone to introduce themselves and tell what we did. I kept praying, "Oh, God, should I say it? Should I tell them I had an abortion?" I was the only black there, and I was like, "How are they going to look at me?" Then it just came out. I remember saying to them, "I probably know more about this than any of you do because I had an abortion." I started crying and so did the woman sitting next to me. I found out later that two other women there had abortions too. They told me in secret and said they could never have done what I did, told about it. I said, "I sure didn't expect to!"

The leader told me then about their postabortion counseling group, and I went to that. It helped. Although we were all different, from different backgrounds, it didn't matter there. Whether we were rich or poor, black or white, we all had done the same thing. It helped a lot, and I thank God for that group, but what I really wanted was to talk to my baby and say, "I'm sorry."

There really wasn't one time when I realized suddenly that I was forgiven. I've just come to it slowly, and I'm still coming to it. Last Sunday in church I was looking at the cross, and I thought, "You have to truly remember that God has forgiven you. That's what you have to do when the guilt is there." I have to tell myself that God has really forgiven me and that I'm the only one that keeps putting this guilt back on my shoulders.

I think it's very hard for any woman who has had an abortion not to blame herself. All the women in the group were dealing with guilt, but who do we blame? Do we blame our husbands, the doctors? I tell them that I blame myself. Even though my husband didn't really want the baby, it was inside me, and he couldn't get it out. It was me that made the decision. I was the one who signed the papers and had the abortion. I have to take the blame for that. It would probably be easier if I could blame someone else, but I can't.

I know I'm forgiven. It's just accepting that God says, "You are forgiven, I love you." Sometimes I feel almost as if it's too bad a sin to be forgiven for, but it's not.

In some ways it's as if the baby never existed. If I had a death certificate or something I could hold onto and cry over—but I don't. That's hard to deal with, that I have absolutely nothing.

One day when I was driving to the mall where I shop, I noticed some people picketing in front of an abortion clinic, and I was impressed. I thought, "That's great. Somebody should do that." Then, another day, I saw a group of them praying. I thought, "I'll pull over and pray with them." When I got up to the group, I realized they weren't praying. They were talking to a 16-year-old girl who was going to have an abortion. Suddenly it just came out. I told her, "I had an abortion; I know what it's like."

That experience made me realize that I can make a difference. I can use what happened to me for other girls to learn from, to realize that you don't have to do this.

I came back the next Saturday and the next one. Finally I became a member of the group. They asked me to take their training, so that's how I got involved in that. I do mostly picketing and sidewalk counseling, and that helps me a lot, to be able to warn somebody what can happen. They don't always listen, but at least I told them.

Now I've started a group called Blacks for Life, and I counsel at the crisis pregnancy center. With my picketing and sidewalk counseling, it all takes a lot of time. Right now I'm helping to organize a Life Chain (in which hundreds of people join hands to protest abortion).

My kids are now in high school. Both of them will be going to college soon, and I'm really going to miss them. When you've had an abortion, you have a very close relationship with your kids. They're my best friends. They still don't know. I think that once they get married and are adults I will tell them, but I don't know. Maybe it's too much to accept the fact that their mother had an abortion, especially because they think abortion is so wrong.

I'm much more open with my kids about sex than my parents were with me. I can say that my daughter is a virgin, and I'm very proud of that. We sit and talk a lot, and they see so much going on today, kids in their classes who have a child, or even more than one.

What has come out of this whole experience for me is number one, I know that following God's word to the letter is the best thing.

When I had my abortion I didn't know God, so I couldn't go to him. So another thing I've learned is that no matter how bad your situation is, no matter how dark and dreary it may seem, it can always change for the better, and God has a purpose.

Even though I've gone through a hard time, it will all work to his glory. Because of my abortion, I can go out and tell others, "You don't have to do this."

ALEXIS: *I knew he would hug me and tell me
that everything was ok, but it really wasn't*

**I looked for sympathy, but there was none, for comforters,
but I found none. (Psalm 69:20)**

*it's OK he said
then hugged me tight
like it really was
it's OK he said
but it wasn't*

*how can it be okay
when they take away
your baby in a jar*

*it looked like I had no choice
it seemed the only way
two little ones already
how could I have another
it's OK he said
but it wasn't*

*they talked real nice
of course you've got no choice
why at your age and
at your income
how can you have one more
it's OK they said
but it wasn't*

*they called my name
and showed me in
antiseptic, neat, and swift
—I was crying—
and then they carried out that jar
it's OK I tried to say
but it wasn't*

*how can it be okay
babies don't belong
in jars*

*I know my child
words can't bring your baby back
hugs won't do the trick
"OK" won't ease the pain
or make you whole again
you bought the lie
and paid for it
with tears and pain
you thought it through
but not enough to save a life
it's done now
but not over*

*they try to comfort you
and tell you it's okay
not really knowing you
and all your tears
the deep ache and shame inside
the price tag of the death
contained within that jar*

*but I know well
the price of sin and shame
I paid it all once long ago
an ugly tortured death
nailed on a cross
for everyone
for you*

*and I know well
what shame is all about
I hung there naked and despised
the butt of jokes and jeers
the object of my Father's wrath*

I bore it all in my own flesh
for everyone
for you

I feel with you
I long for you
I waited patiently
through your long pain and tears
and now I'll comfort you
I'll dry your tears and ease your pain
I'll take away your shame

for I've taken that whole mess
and wrapped it up within my death
and now it's disappeared
I've got more for you
than just a hug
take eat and drink
my body and my blood
the price I paid in death
the gift I give for life
your death in me
my life in you
you're forgiven clean and new
what happened to your sin?
it's not "OK"
it's gone

Paula

Paula describes herself as "Miss Goody Two-Shoes," the girl who grew up always obeying the rules, always being "good." During college, however, she drifted farther and farther from God and her "good-girl" ideals. Living with her boyfriend after graduation seemed like the ultimate rebellion, and she enjoyed "playing house" until an unplanned pregnancy made reality very clear.

Urged by her boyfriend, who didn't want to be tied down to a baby, she had an abortion. She knew it was the wrong decision even as she left the clinic. Later, the births of each of her three children made the pain and guilt even worse.

Finally realizing, nearly ten years later, that God had forgiven her has helped ease the guilt but not the pain. She longs for a memorial to aborted babies where women could come and grieve, the way people who have lost a loved one do at the Vietnam War memorial. "I'd like to see my baby's name carved in a stone wall," she says. "But there's no such place for us."

† † † † †

I grew up in a small town of 500, on a working farm. We had sheep, lambs, horses, chickens, ducks—the whole works. It was an ideal place to grow up. We worked hard but we had fun, too. I have three younger brothers and one older sister. We're all very close in age, from 11 months to two years apart. They are all still on farms. I'm the only one who isn't.

My parents took us to church and Sunday school every Sunday. It was a small church. My parents were not happy there. It didn't seem to be a very close-knit church. When the service was over, people would leave. There wasn't much socializing or getting to know each other. There was nothing to keep you going all week long. You just went to church, came home and forgot about it, and the next week went again. It didn't really do anything for me. I watched Billy Graham and the other television preachers often, but that wasn't staying with me either. I guess I was looking for God somehow, and, although he was there, I didn't know it.

I wasn't close to my father. He was always out working on the farm. He just wasn't there very much. He was a strict German and grew up in the tradition that you keep your feelings to yourself—you don't talk about things; you just live. I had a somewhat closer relationship with my mother, but we still didn't talk. We did a lot of stuff together—canning, shopping. We never argued, but we didn't talk either.

I didn't date in high school—never went on a date until college. I was shy and quiet, and I remember feeling rather embarrassed that I was never asked out. I went to a few football games, and that was about it. When you live on a farm, your life is different; you just come home and do your work. You don't do much running around. My brothers and sister all got married at age 16 or 17 (in all but one case the girl was pregnant), and I thought I would grow up to be a farm wife too. That's what was expected of me, and I really never thought of anything else. But then a neighbor lady urged me to go to college.

When I went off to college, church kind of stopped for me. I went once or twice to the campus church, but then I just stopped going. I was suddenly free to do what I wanted to do, and I didn't want to go to church. When I came home I'd go to church with my parents, but when I went back to school, that was it.

I didn't become sexually active nearly as early as my brothers and sister did. Maybe I saw what my brothers and sister were doing and thought it was wrong. Maybe my parent's values were still strong in me then, but in college things change. You do what everyone else is doing. I wasn't strong enough to keep those values. I'd never drunk before, but I started in college because that's what everyone else was doing. Everyone in the wing partied, and so I did too. I became sexually active, but I wasn't very experienced. I just had sex twice, with one boy.

There were a few boys I dated, but no one I was really interested in until winter of my sophomore year when I met Jerry. There was just something about him. I thought, "I want to meet that guy." He didn't really notice me at first, but there was something about him that attracted me. I came home from our first date and told the girls in my wing that I was going to marry him! Maybe I just made up my mind that I was going to make it happen. I don't know because it was pretty rocky all the years I dated him. He caused me so much grief. He wasn't ready to settle down.

I remember one incident the summer after my sophomore year. I wanted to have a big party at the farm for my birthday and invite all my college friends. Jerry was in a band, and they were going to play. My parents said we could serve beer. The party was in full swing. There was a lot of drinking going on. I had gotten quite drunk, and my mother found me asleep on my bed with Jerry. She was just horrified and went to get my dad. By the time he got there, I had awakened. Dad walked into my room with the fly swatter! He didn't hit Jerry, but he threw him out of the house. Obviously they didn't like him very much and didn't want me to see him again. Somehow everyone in the whole town found out about it, so it was very embarrassing for me. I was the black sheep of the family for a while.

But I continued seeing Jerry. Sometimes when I felt like he was treating me badly—I'd see him with somebody else—I'd come home and want to talk to my mother about it, but we never did.

By the end of my junior year I decided that I wasn't going to see him any more, that I just couldn't take it. I started dating another boy. We were mainly just friends who spent time together. One time when we were going swimming, Jerry came over and went along with us. He got very jealous that I was with this other guy, and it seemed like that's what made him realize that I was what he wanted. So we got back together.

During my senior year, Jerry told me he loved me. I couldn't believe what I was hearing—I made him say it again!

School ended, I graduated. Jerry had a job in a medium-sized town not too far from home. He asked me to live with him there. My first response was, "I don't think I can do that." I remember when a cousin of mine lived with her boyfriend, how upset everyone in my family was with her. I thought my parents would be fit to be tied; but Jerry kind of put it that if I didn't stay there with him, he didn't know what would happen to us. I was too insecure to take that chance. I told my parents I was moving to look for a teaching job. I felt so guilty.

Finally I told my mother over the phone that I was living with Jerry. She put my father on the phone. I remember his words to this day. He told me, "You are sinning," but I did it anyway. I didn't know what else to do. I didn't want to move back home. I wanted to be with Jerry, but he didn't want to get married. He said he loved me, but he wasn't quite sure.

As soon as I moved in, I got pregnant, probably that

same week. Why I wasn't using any birth control, I don't remember. I guess it was because the pill had done some weird things to my body, so I stopped taking it.

It was fun playing house at first. I worked for our landlord, making picture frames. That's how I guessed I was pregnant. I was working with him in the basement and got very nauseated. I ran upstairs, feeling like I was going to throw up. I drove into the next town for a pregnancy test. It was positive.

I wish now I had called my mother and told her, but I was too afraid that she'd say, "It's all your fault; your actions caused this." I didn't want to hear that. If I'd called her, there would have been no way I'd have had an abortion, but I didn't tell her.

Jerry kept saying, "There's no way I want a baby now. I just started life. I can't handle this." I was only 21; he was 23. I didn't know what to do. I realized I was pregnant at the end of June. I carried it around for nearly six weeks, trying to decide what to do. Things weren't good between Jerry and me. We couldn't talk; I felt totally lost. I went into a church one morning and just sat there, thinking I'd find an answer. But nothing happened. No answer came to me.

Sometimes I felt like I really wanted to end it all for myself. I remember thinking, "I'd like to just jump off a bridge and not have to make this decision." But I couldn't do that. I did talk to one woman, a Christian. I don't remember where I got her name, or if she was a professional counselor or just someone who tried to convince women not to have abortions. I didn't think she was much help, and I never called her back.

Jerry and I were having terrible fights. He'd say, "It's not a baby. It's only this big." At one point I left, saying "I can't stay here. I can't handle this." I thought I could do it all on my own, that I didn't need anyone else; but I came back.

I really didn't know what to do. I went to a department

store and looked at baby clothes and furniture and maternity clothes, and checked the prices. I kept wishing Jerry
would say, "Forget it; let's just have the baby." But he never
did.

I went to a doctor, and I thought, "If she can hear a
heartbeat, then I won't have an abortion." She couldn't
hear it; it was too early. That afternoon while riding
behind Jerry on his motorcycle I told him, "I'm going to do
it. I'm going to have the abortion." I felt such a sense of
relief that the decision was made and I knew what I was
going to do.

We made the appointment.

I remember going to the clinic. I told Jerry I wasn't going
alone, that he had to come with me. I remember driving
up to the clinic and seeing all these people outside it, carrying signs. I don't know if my mind was gone or what, but
I walked right past them. I walked in.

The first step was an explanation of what was going to
happen. Then I went into the procedure room. Now I
wonder why didn't I just walk out of there and let them
keep my 200 dollars, but I didn't. I do remember that the
nurses were very nice to me. I kept telling myself it was
just another operation, like having an appendix out. You
just go in and have it done. The doctor was very cold. His
attitude was "Next!"

I remember on the way out seeing the other women in
the waiting room and thinking, "My God, you don't know
what you're in for."

I remember Jerry and I walking out to the car. There
was a trash can behind the clinic. A nurse walked out of
the clinic and threw a bag into the trash can. I thought,
"My baby is in that bag, being thrown into the trash." It
probably wasn't of course, but all I could think was that
they had taken my baby and thrown it in the trash.

I knew right away that I had made a mistake, that this

was the most awful thing that could ever happen to anybody. Jerry and I both sat in the car and cried. He told me
later that it made him realize how much he loved me, and
he wished that it hadn't happened. But it was too late for
that. He took me out for dinner that night. I wondered
what we were celebrating.

I cried an awful lot in the weeks right after. I'd see a diaper
commercial or a pregnant woman or a baby and I'd cry.

We decided to get married. A few months before the
wedding, I thought I was pregnant again. A home pregnancy test was positive. I don't know if I just wished it to
be so much that I created the symptoms or what. I only
remember that I was so excited. I thought, "In two months
I'll be married. I don't care what anyone thinks. There's no
way this one is going." But then I got my period. I don't
know if it was a miscarriage or a regular period; but I
remember thinking, "I took one of God's away; now he's
taking one of mine away."

Then we got married, and nine months later I was pregnant. Once I had my son, I felt even worse. After I saw
him, I could only think that he had a brother or sister
somewhere who was only two years older than he was.
How could I have done that? That never went away. I
never told anyone; I never talked about it.

We moved to another city. We had two more children,
little girls. With each new baby the grief would start up all
over again.

We started going to church again, but I still didn't really
have God in my life. I remember one Sunday about a year
after we joined the church when, after the service, the
pastor was doing a program on abortion. I sat in the back
of the church with my three little kids, watching and
thinking, "If only he knew, what would he think?" I
remember thinking that I should be up there, telling people what abortion is really like, but I couldn't. I didn't want

anyone to know.

I thought, "Here I am, Miss Goody Two-Shoes all my life, and then I go and screw it up so badly." I'd done so many things wrong, so many things I never thought I would do. And I didn't know why.

I didn't think God loved me. I'd pray for forgiveness, but I never felt it. I didn't feel like God was in my life at all, and I didn't see how he could forgive any woman for doing what I had done. I wished I could talk to the pastor about it, but I was afraid.

However, I finally did call him. I didn't tell him what it was about because I didn't know what I was going to say. When I told him what I had done, he wasn't floored by it at all, and he assured me that my sin was forgiven. I was so worried about that baby: "Where is it? Is it anywhere? Will it be in heaven when I get there?" The pastor told me that he and his wife had lost a baby through miscarriage and that they had also wondered where it was. He told me that it was the same no matter how the babies died, and he felt sure they are in heaven. Although the Bible doesn't speak on it, he believes that God will keep those babies with him.

I felt an enormous sense of relief. For the first time, I felt that I was truly forgiven. It didn't make the hurt or the pain go away, but it did lessen it. I found that I could manage to not think about it all the time. I began to believe that I will see that baby someday. In my heart I feel that he or she is in heaven waiting for me, but it still hurts.

I'll never forget the day I had the abortion, August 7th, for the rest of my life. I remember one August 7th when Jerry and I were driving somewhere in the car. I was thinking about that baby and found myself wishing that there were someplace where all us women who have had abortions could go: A place where there could be a memorial for all those babies, a tombstone like they have for veterans. A place where we could go and put down our flowers, just like in a normal death. A place where I could have "Baby X" carved in the stone. A place where I could go on that day and just pour it all out if I wanted to. But there's no such place for us to grieve. We certainly can't go back to the abortion clinic.

It's been ten years now. I think I've changed a lot in those ten years. God is playing a greater role in my life now than he ever has before. For so many years I was so busy being a mom, so busy at church, but I couldn't seem to find God. Now I'm finding him again. I've realized the importance of prayer; I'm coming closer to him.

My kids are school age now, and I know how important it is to teach them what is right and wrong. I talk about things with them, much more than I ever did with my parents. We talk about God and how he is a part of their lives. I hope they never have to make a decision like this, but if they do I'm trying to teach them to make the right one. If one of my daughters ever got pregnant, first I'd cry. Then I'd pray that I'd say the right things to her. I don't know how I would go about it, but I would tell her that we love her and that God still loves her. I would tell her that that baby will love her, even if she gave it up for adoption. I think I'd have to share my experience with her, but I don't know if I could do it. It would be very hard. I'd get some help—counselors and pastors—to help us get through it. I'd tell her right out that abortion is not the right decision. But I hope by talking to my children now and keeping the lines of communication open, that that will never be necessary.

My mom died a few years ago; I never told her about the abortion. I'm much closer to my dad now, but I don't think I could ever tell him either. I'd feel like some of the burden would be off me if I could, but on the other hand it would be such a burden to him. Sometimes we talk about abortion in general, and I feel so two-faced.

I feel like my Mom is already in heaven, and she knows now what I went through, and I feel like she's taking care of that grandchild for me. I know that's just a fantasy, but it makes me feel as if the burden of telling her has been lifted.

The whole experience has had an effect on our marriage, but I wouldn't say it has drawn us closer together. Jerry doesn't talk about it much. If I need to cry and talk about it, he is always willing to listen, even though I think he feels somewhat uncomfortable with it. He says that he didn't really think it was real. He thought it was just a fetus, just a group of cells, not really a baby.

There were times when I've thought, "I did this all for Jerry," and I've almost hated him. There were even times when I wanted to hurt him back in the same way he hurt me. But then I'd think, "But it wasn't his fault. It was my decision, my sin. I can't blame him."

In some ways it seems such a long time ago. I still feel bad; I still feel sorry; I still cry sometimes, but not as much as I used to. If I hadn't gotten the assurance from my pastor that God has forgiven me, I think I'd be a basket case now.

If I've learned anything in this experience, it's that there really is a God, a God who cares. There is forgiveness for what I've done and what every other woman who has had an abortion has done. In God we can find that forgiveness and release that guilt. I wish I could say that to all those millions of women who have had abortions, that God is there, and they can find forgiveness and peace in him.

To someone who is considering an abortion I can only say, "Don't do it. You will regret it in some way for the rest of your life." The thought will always be there that you've done this to that little baby, and those babies are real. You might be young and scared and lonely, but that baby is God's child and deserves a chance to live.

PAULA: *there's no place for us to grieve*

**How long must I wrestle with my thoughts and
every day have sorrow in my heart? (Psalm 13:2)**

*when you mourn
you should have
at least a name
to remember
you should have
at least a face
to recall
you should have
at least a stone
to visit
where you can cry your tears
and feel the hurt inside*

*but with me it's not that way
my baby had no name, you see
it has no grave
it did have life
but now no more
because
I took its life away
and now it's gone*

*and so
I weep and cry
but I cannot mourn
not really
not suitably
because
there is no face
on this grief of mine
and
there is no grave
no place to go
to cry my tears
and mourn my loss
where do you go
to mourn*

*when there is no grave?
where do you go
to cry
your tears
to feel
your pain
to tell
your grief?*

*hear me, child
I'll hear your pain
I'll feel your grief
I'll mourn with you*

*I know full well
the horrid feel
of tears in throat
the aching hole
deep down inside
of loss and grief combined*

*Gethsemane they called that place
I called it hell
for there I felt the tempter's power
there I bore the weight of sin
and with that weight, its pain and
    grief
your pain, you see
your grief as well
I'll mourn with you
I too have no grave, you know
for I am risen
from my tomb*

baptized into my death and grave
your sin is gone
for all your pain and grief
are mine
baptized into my Easter joy
your life has come
for all my virtue and delight
are yours

you have a share in me
and in my life
which has no end
so come, my child
now dry your tears
and live with me

Dee

Dee just celebrated her 63d birthday. She's a striking woman with elegant, high cheekbones and long, gray-streaked blond hair piled high on her head. Huge, colorful hoops swing at her ears, adding a note of youthful glee.

It's been more than 40 years since Dee had her abortion. The ghost of that baby, she says, lived in her marriage and her relationships with her children until just a few years ago.

A product of a dysfunctional family herself, Dee retreated into alcoholism and nearly destroyed her marriage and her relationship with her children.

But God heals, and he uses tools—in Dee's case psychotherapy plus the training to be a postabortion counselor—to bring his healing.

He has healed Dee. She doesn't know how many years of life she has left—it could be a few; it could be 20 or more—but she is using them productively. She's walking proof that you are never too old to grow.

† † † † †

I was born in a Michigan town on the Canadian border. My grandparents were immigrants, half from Finland and half from Ireland. None of them spoke English.

I was the oldest of five children. My family was happy, energetic, lazy—and violent. We had a lot of fun and we laughed a lot because my parents were both spontaneous and high spirited, but there was so much turmoil in my home.

I grew up consciously hating my mother. I was thoroughly beaten about once every two weeks, although I don't have any bitterness over that because I was sassy and defiant to her every single day of my life. It was like a battle to the death—she would like to have breathed for me if she could have: just totally dominant. She was very religious, played the organ at church, and her father was a lay preacher. Her parents used to stay up all night, praying and rejoicing with some sort of Finnish apostolic group. There's mental illness, alcoholism, suicide, and murder in her family. She's really the only survivor—if you define that as someone who lived a fairly functional life and lived past middle age—in that family.

My father was a happy Irish drunk. Every payday and on every special occasion he would get drunk. I thought it was wonderful as a child because he was always happy, telling stories and singing Irish songs. My parents' whole marriage was like worlds colliding. They both were strong, dominant personalities.

The other kids must have learned to get smart around my parents, because I was the only one they beat. I never did learn, when they asked, "Did you do this?" not to say yes. I'm not sorry about it though. It did teach me a respect for authority.

We were a religious family, very strict, always went to church; but I wouldn't say I was a Christian as a child. All going to church did for me was to give me some Scripture verses I memorized and give me a pastor and his wife who were like angels for me. They cared about me and gave me a lot of guidance.

I tried my whole adult life, before my parents died, to confront them and talk to them about our family, but I never could. I remember once saying to myself, "I don't think Mother will ever understand thing one," but by the end of her life it seemed OK to me. By then I'd become a Christian, and I'd changed. She lived with us at the end, and I took care of her. It was a good thing. Even then she was a terrible person to get along with, but I was filled with God's grace and could do it.

I started dating when I was 12. It wasn't a kissing kind of dating. It was more that we were the two biggest kids in the junior high! All my girlfriends had dumped me because I had boobs, but he was my friend. We had so many interests in common; he's the one who introduced me to opera. It was wonderful. We're still friends.

I dated all the time in high school. I once had three dates in one weekend. That was during the war years. There were 30,000 service men in our town of 18,000, but I was not allowed to date them. I wasn't sexually active then, oh, never. I never even held hands with most of the boys I dated. I had a sense, an ego strength about me that said, "I'm not giving myself away to just anybody."

I left home at 18 and went to Wisconsin to go to college, majoring in music and English. My parents could never have afforded to send me; but I'd saved money from my job working in the post office, and I got a scholarship.

At the end of my junior year I dropped out for a while to earn money. My brother had gotten married at 17, and they had a baby shortly after. My mother said, "Poor Bud, you've got to go to Washington D.C. to take care of them." I never asked why, I just got on a plane and went.

Then I got a job as a teacher in a country school up in the north woods—you could do that without a degree in those days. I taught second grade. That's when I lost my virginity. There was this hillbilly-type person, but he was very sweet. He told me at the beginning of the year, "I'm going to seduce you." I just laughed thinking, "I've come through the ranks, fellah, you're not going to do anything."

But at the end of the year I gave in. I liked him, although I knew I was never going to marry him.

Once that gate is open . . . well, I went through a period when I had one-time things with all my old boyfriends. I was so mad at my mother because she had always told me that God would strike me dead if I did this, but I never believed that. I felt God knew how driven I was. I was really a party girl. Marriage looked so bad to me (my mother always said, "Don't marry young because once you're married it's all over") that I thought I needed to have my fun first.

I never even thought about birth control. I don't think anybody used anything back then. Condoms were the only choice; I didn't even know what a diaphragm was. But I didn't get pregnant.

Then I came back to finish college. I met my husband the first weekend after I started. My geology lab partner set up a blind date for me. On our second date I knew this was the man I wanted to marry. I was 23; Howard was a year and a half younger.

I got pregnant about the first time or two we ever had sex. I was very happy, but scared because you just didn't do those things then. I thought, "This is wonderful." I felt good, never nauseated. Then I told Howard.

He didn't really say much, but he came back a week later with a name and phone number. He didn't ask me. He just said, "I'll get the money, and we'll go and get you an abortion." I was a such a non-assertive person at that time. I was used to accommodating myself to people who were hard to live with, so I went along with it.

It was the simplest thing in the world. Howard asked one of his fraternity brothers, whose girlfriend had recently had an abortion, where to go, and he got a name from him. The name was a doctor in a small town nearby. We drove there, but the doctor said he didn't do abortions, but he would give us the name of someone who did. That's how secret it was in those days. The doctor was in Chicago. We went there on a Saturday. We had strict directions. It was all very furtive. Howard was to drive me up to the door and not to come into the house. "Get out of here, and don't come back for two hours," the doctor said. We paid cash in advance, $350.

The doctor had a small operating room in his house—it was sort of like a dentist's chair, if I remember right. He used a general anesthetic on me. I got through it by being a somnambulist. It was like I was out of body, like I departed; I just wasn't there.

I think now that a part of me died then, and I'm just getting myself back in my old age. It isn't that I didn't respond fully to life—I did. I'm the kind who is willing to tear into stuff. I get involved. But it was like something in me hardened, and I had a tough heart. When you kill somebody that's what happens. There is a cost.

We got married six months later. I remember a friend asked me to play for her wedding. I'd never played a big pipe organ with foot pedals before, and I was scared to do it. So I said to Howard, "I don't want to play for this wedding. Let's get married instead." That's how flippant we were.

We got married in his family's living room. I was wearing a navy blue, strapless lace dress with a little bolero, and I bought my own wedding ring. I never got an engagement ring until about eight years ago. For our honeymoon we drove to my parents' house in Upper Michigan and painted their kitchen for them!

We lived with his parents for the first year, and I got pregnant instantly. I was teaching in a high school and directing a choir, and I was about nine weeks pregnant, when one day after school I went into labor. I was in labor all night, but Howard didn't call a doctor or even tell his parents. It was like we were ashamed of it. Something yucky was happening, and we didn't want to admit it. I was too weak to teach for a few days afterward; I was really so alone. Six months later I was cutting the grass with a push mower, when I suddenly started hemorrhaging; but I was still afraid to say anything. I just didn't think at that time that I had any rights.

In 1950 Howard joined the Navy so he wouldn't be drafted into the Korean war. We moved to Washington D.C. for his training. We got an apartment, and I got a job as a dental assistant, because I couldn't get a teaching job mid-year. I got pregnant again and lost that baby at 13 weeks. I went to a university and read everything I could find on abortion and miscarriage, and I couldn't find anything at that time that linked them. Now, of course, they are beginning to report a connection.

I never really suffered any distress after the abortion until I lost those two babies. Then I think I should have been hospitalized with depression; but I'm a fighter, and what I did was become an alcoholic instead. I come from a drinking culture, and I'd done a lot of drinking in college—everybody did. I just began drinking more.

In the next years we moved a lot—eight times in two years. When Howard got out of the service, we moved back to where his family lived. I got pregnant again. I was always in danger of losing it, but I really, really wanted that baby, and he did too. I remember walking around thinking that I had to concentrate, to hold that baby in by sheer force of will.

When our daughter was born, I had a rocking chair ready for her, but she stuck her elbow out and held her head up and wouldn't let me cuddle her. I felt like there was something so terribly wrong with me, that a baby would see right through me. She had these great big, penetrating blue eyes, and she'd look at me, and I'd think,

"She sees right into my soul." I knew that wasn't reasonable, but that's how I felt. It had a big effect on how I related to her.

I needed to get pregnant again right away. I could not rest until I had three children. I realize now it was the two I lost plus the abortion, but I didn't see that then. I had three babies in 32 months and another one a few years later.

During all the years of our marriage, Howard and I never had one fight. He's an extremely nice man, a real gentleman, and very passive. I would characterize our marriage as uneventful—he had his business, and I had the kids. But I had this undercurrent of great anger that I never recognized. I think now it came from the abortion.

I was still doing a lot of drinking. I remember when the children were little, there was a young woman who lived up the street from me. We'd get together, with her five kids and my four. They'd play, and we'd drink. I was never a falling-down drunk. I did my job. I was never neglectful of my children; they were always important to me. But I drank and drank and drank. I could carry a lot. I just wasn't dealing with my anger.

I began getting involved in some stuff that we would now call "New Age." I was into Transcendental Meditation and some kind of hokey spiritual support group. I was really searching, but at that time I didn't know any Christians. One of my first pastors after I became a Christian said, "You can find some good meat in any garbage can," and I did have some spiritual growth during that time. I looked everywhere. I sang and played in many different churches (I was paid for that), and I heard everything. By the time I became a Christian, I'd tried every bridge. I knew it was this or nothing. I was dead if this wasn't it—but I knew it was.

While I was becoming more and more unhappy,

Howard's business was failing, and we were going bankrupt. One Saturday I told my husband that I hated him; it would take a miracle to save our marriage; and I wanted to leave him. I took the youngest, who was still a baby, and went to a nearby school and sat on the steps and just rocked. I felt like all the starch had gone out of me. I remember the thought coming into my mind, "Not my will but thine be done," but I wasn't sure what it meant.

On Monday someone Howard worked with stopped by and invited him to a Bible study for Christian business-men. He went, and there he heard men speak about Christ as if he were alive, and that was shocking to him. A couple of men asked him if he had any problems, and he blurted out that he was going bankrupt and his wife wanted to divorce him and he couldn't sleep. They told him that he wasn't built to carry all those problems, that he should turn his problems over to God and let God help him. He was desperate enough to do that.

He came home that night and stood in the door with the sun behind him and told me about God. At first I didn't listen, but a few days later I realized that was the one thing I hadn't tried in my life. God came into my life like a gift. He gave me love for my husband again, and I no longer wanted to divorce him. I stopped drinking that same day. We poured about $75 worth of liquor down the sink that night.

I realized right away that I was forgiven for the abor-tion. I remember thinking, "There's a blackboard up there that's been totally wiped clean, and all my sins are forgot-ten forever." But, though I had been delivered from my guilt by salvation, I had not dealt with the traumatic effects of the abortion, which were buried very, very deep.

One Sunday about five years ago I was sitting in church reading the bulletin, when, down at the bottom, I saw this line: "Anyone interested in counseling postabortion

women, call this number." There were 14 women who
responded; we all went to a training course. All but two of
those women had had an abortion. The training was wonderful. The leader, who was a nurse and had an abortion
herself, helped us a lot. It was really a therapy group for
us.

My moment of truth came when, after I'd told my story,
one of the women asked, "What are you feeling right
now?" Before thinking, I blurted out, "Grief." And I realized that was it—I had grieved for my two miscarriages,
but I had never grieved the abortion. I had just tried to put
it out of my mind. Forty years later I finally was in touch
with it. It wasn't as overwhelming as it might have been,
because I didn't have to deal with the guilt. That was over;
but I had to face the damage in my marriage, in my relationships, as a result of that abortion. I had to face how
self-destructive, how driven, I had been. It was awful to sit
there and face the anger.

I know that baby is in heaven; I know I will see it again.
I've grieved now for that baby, and for the real marriage
Howard and I could have had for all those years, instead of
having ghosts walking. And with that came healing.

Today I feel more alive than I ever have. I have more
reality in my relationships than I've ever had. When I was
such an angry person and was so driven, my children
hated me, just like I'd hated my mother. I couldn't figure
that out because I didn't do to them what she did to me,
but I think they hated my driveness. Now I've had a loos-
ening and a letting go. My kids like me now. They even
love me!

With my husband, it's been a renaissance. It's like all the
layers are being peeled away and we're getting down to
the real stuff. We talk about real things now.

I know we have years of productive life left, and we're
becoming more and more productive people. I've been

teaching violin full time for two years. I was afraid to try that before. Howard is starting over with a new business. Our life has been reduced to poverty in a way, but it's like we've been stripped of all the phony baggage and are beginning to live on purpose and to relate in reality, not through all the ghosts. It's very exciting.

I have more optimism and feel better physically than I ever have in my life. I used to be afraid, confused, full of pain in my body from all the anger. The turn-around started the day I read that ad about postabortion counseling.

I'm not formally involved in that kind of counseling right now. I'm beginning to feel that I'm too far removed in age from the young women—they relate to me like a grandmother. They are so raw and so hurting. They don't get as much from me because I'm so much older; but I'm always there on call if someone wants to talk to me, and I've been leading a support group at church for people with alcohol problems.

I know now there's an answer to problems. People need to have that knowledge in their pocket, that Christ gives them hope. I also really think it's important for people to see an old lady like me growing in her old age!

DEE: *a part of me died then*

**Blessed is he whose transgressions are forgiven,
whose sins are covered. (Psalm 32:1)**

*we lived together, he and I
in perfect wedded bliss
the perfect man, the perfect wife
a perfect home, and perfect kids
the picture of perfection
but it was only sham
forty years we lived together married
we've been man and wife for five*

*walking ghosts we were
going through the motions
living out our fears
playing out our script
haunted by the ghosts of childhood
lonely specters from our past
images of pain and hurt
buried deep within our hearts
camouflaged in daily life's routine
hidden under shallow laughter*

*I learned to live with pain
liquid anesthetic from a bottle
numbed the ache and veiled the hurt
but it lingered underneath
engraved upon my heart
the hurt and pain remained
inscribed both hard and deep*

*hatred is like fire
consuming everything within its path
anger eats you up inside
I played the game and acted out
   my part
a paragon of virtue:
calm, at peace, serene
but anger gnawed away at me
a volcano churned continually inside*

*welling up from time to time
all that ugly pent-up anger
spilling out upon the innocent*

*that child was victim of our anger
an avalanche of pain and hurt
a lava flow of anger
welling up and pouring out
we took that life
and now it's gone
a casualty of misplaced anger*

*we covered very nicely
took on our roles
played out our parts
husband, wife, and parents
but it was all a sham
going through the motions
walking ghosts we were
haunted by the nightmares
out of our frightful past*

*one silent ghost stood stubbornly
refusing to be banished
the painful memory of that tiny one
whose life we took
the silent victim of our sin
our little casualty*

*come near, my child
now hear me carefully
I play no games
I act no part
I am straight and real
now is the time
the time for truth*

you played the game of let's pretend
you masqueraded well
yet all the while
beneath those roles you played
hid sin and guilt and grief

that tiny silent casualty
was my own creation
the life I gave
you took
this is the ugly truth
but I am the truth as well
the way
the life
so hear me now
and listen carefully
my word brings life to you
my way dispenses freedom
my truth means liberation
from the bitter bonds of memory
that tiny silent figure
the phantom from your past
the memory of your sin
and deeper still, your guilt

I bore that guilt you see
and bore it all away with me
into my death
which is your life
that cross of mine
the place of truth
the truth of sins confessed
the truth of sins absolved
in my own body and my blood
shed once for you
and here and now
for you to eat and drink
the pledges of my promise sure

in me you're clean and whole
free to live
and free to love
my love for you

my life in you
and now in me you're free
so come and live in me

Jeanine

Jeanine has, by her own admission, a long way to go in her struggle to reconcile her past with her present, to forgive herself for some of the things she's done, in the same way that she knows God has forgiven her. She does know that, but her past, including her three abortions, still haunts her. She sobs as she tells her story, sometimes to the point of not being able to talk.

Jeanine and her sisters, who were an important influence in her life, grew up in an industrial suburb of a large, Midwestern city, a town of blue-collar factory workers with a tavern on nearly every corner. Her family appeared to be religious. Church on Sunday and parochial school were a big part of her growing up. Yet there was a dark undercurrent in her family: attempted sexual abuse, extramarital affairs, multiple divorces.

Jeanine covers her pain with laughter. She has an alter ego, a clown named Chuckles, who wears big floppy shoes with pom poms, a polka dot suit, and shocking pink hair, and volunteers to entertain at hospitals and nursing homes.

The clown and the pain—the two sides of Jeanine. Even when she's describing the most painful things in her life, she laughs; but when she is Chuckles, she doesn't paint her nose red in the fashion of most clowns. That, she says, is because her nose is usually red anyway. From crying.

† † † † †

I guess I was a pretty "ho-hum" kid most of the time. There were some happy times—we used to go camping a lot and get together for big family holidays. There were also a lot of times when I and my three sisters were left to our own devices, to just pass the time away.

In their own way, I think my parents loved me. They weren't real demonstrative, but I don't think I ever doubted that they loved me. Sex was a closed topic in our family. I remember my mother taking me to the school basement one night to see that movie, *What Happens when Girls Get Older*, or something like that; but I never really discussed anything much at home. I suppose that, after their other three daughters, my parents were just glad to get a quiet one! I was extremely shy. We'd go to my aunt and uncle's house, and I'd stay in the car. It took me a long time to get over that. Maybe now I've gone the other way!

My parents were quite religious. My father was baptized as an adult, but I always felt that I took my religion for granted. I went to parochial school, but I always did as much as I could to get out of doing memory work!

I had some crazy experiences in early grade school. I remember playing "Show and Tell" with the little boy down the street. My mother didn't take it real well. She chased me down the alley with a paint stick! I had a couple of experiences with an older cousin—curious kids. One boy tried to get me to "do it" with him on the school bus, although it didn't go very far. I guess I was just curious, always ready to try something new, even though I knew it was wrong. I think I had a lot of questions, and no one ever really sat down and talked to me about them.

Some of my experiences crossed the line into sexual abuse. When my second oldest sister was married, I would baby-sit for her kids while she and my mom were at choir practice. A couple of times my brother-in-law made advances. I really don't remember how far he went, but I know he pinned me up against the wall a couple of times. I remember on his birthday sending him a card. I wrote in it that, now that he was a year older, I hoped he'd act like it. My parents found out about it, and they told him to stop it, and he did.

About a year later I was baby-sitting for my other sister. I stayed overnight, sleeping on the couch. In the middle of the night her husband came down and fondled me, tried to convince me to just relax and enjoy it; but he kept to himself after that. I can't really pinpoint what feelings I had about that. Probably confusion. I don't remember if anger was in there. I know I didn't want to tell anybody.

My sisters never really talked about what they were doing, but I knew some things were going on. One of my nephews was conceived while my sister's husband was out to sea. My other sister just divorced her third husband.

In high school I always wished I had a boyfriend, but I never did. I remember wishing I could find somebody special.

When I was a junior, I had a crush on a guy who was going to graduate, and I was afraid I'd never see him again. I convinced him he should go into the piano practice rooms and "make out" with me; but when he got there, he told me he didn't want to do that with me because I was a nice girl. Inside I was screaming, "I am not! Let me prove it!" I don't know if inside I really didn't think I was a nice girl, or if I didn't want to be. I just know I desperately wanted to go in there with him. He left, and that was the last time I ever saw him. That was as close as I ever came to having a date in high school—and when you have three older sisters with boyfriends, that can be hard.

After high school I went to business school. I met a guy named Bill. He'd come to my house, or I'd go to his house.

We'd go to movies and stuff. We started making out—all the way. I liked him, but I don't know that I really loved him. I broke it off because my mother said the relationship wasn't going anywhere. He really took it hard, but I just did things I was told to at that time. I didn't really think much about them, or try to figure out who I was or what I really wanted. He married a girlfriend of mine, and we're all good friends today.

I moved out of my parents' home when they moved to a nearby small town, and I lived with a girlfriend, going home on weekends. I dated a few guys from the school and had a few short affairs with a couple of married men there. It was just casual—they were nice guys (although it wasn't very nice what they were doing to their wives).

I continued going to church on weekends with my folks. It wasn't easy to rationalize that my religion said, "Thou shalt not," and I was. I just kind of turned it off and on, or I tried to. I remember when I took Communion I crossed my fingers behind my back and said to God, "Please, just hang in there."

I think I just wanted the relationships: to be held and wanted and cared about. I found it wherever I could.

I met my first husband on a blind date. We dated a lot, then I started going up to his apartment. He told me I was the type of woman he wanted as the mother for his kids, so we planned to get married. But I got pregnant. He was very matter-of-fact about it, told me how I was to get it taken care of. He said he wasn't ready for a child yet. I was just scared. I don't think I even argued with him. I was mainly worried about my parents. I thought it would tear them up if they knew.

I don't remember much about the procedure; it was over real quick. I just remember lying on an army cot after and them bundling me up and sending me home. He wasn't even there to pick me up. I took a taxi home. I felt very empty afterward. I definitely needed some counseling or something, but there was no one to give it to me. I blocked out any feelings I had about it. He was still the man I loved, and I still wanted to marry him.

My mother didn't know about the abortion; but she said we were seeing too much of each other, and we should move the wedding date up. So we did.

Right before we got married, he had a failed suicide attempt. The marriage lasted about 15 months. I needed time to grow up and learn how to handle relationships, and he wouldn't give me the time to do it. He just kicked me out, and that was it. He said, "You're young and nice looking. You'll find someone and get married again."

I was totally devastated. I'd given him my love and my trust, and he just threw it all back in my face. I didn't know who I was yet, where I was heading, what I wanted. I went to a counselor briefly, but she didn't really help me very much. She just sort of held my hand while I cried, and that was about it.

I got an apartment and a job. I met this guy down in the basement laundry room, and he ended up moving in and freeloading off me for a while—"bed and breakfast" I guess. At the time, I thought I was falling in love with him too. I was always looking too hard and not finding it. I know I was ashamed of what I was doing because, when my folks came for a visit, I'd usher him into my closet, and he'd sit there while I visited with them. Finally, I lost my job and moved back home, and that was it with him.

About that time I got a CB radio in my car so I could call for help in an emergency, but I used it more for pleasure than for emergency. It got me into a lot of trouble—or rather the mouth connected to the CB did. I started hanging out with truck drivers. I'd go down to a truck stop and hang around, go out dancing and dining with them—and sleeping with them and everything else. Hence, abortion number two. The father was a truck driver, but I don't know which one. I was with a lot of strangers then. Even on the way to visit my sister out west, I jumped into a lot of beds along the way. I was a pretty good wreck about that time, but I still never really sat down and tried to figure out who I was and what I wanted. I still wasn't thinking for myself.

It was like I was leading a double life. I was trying to uphold one end of it and going down the drain on the other. I remember bringing home a couple of truck drivers that I thought I was in love with. One was married, but he kept telling me he was going to get divorced. They were all just using me. Somewhere in there I ended up pregnant for the third time.

The abortions were all alike. You go in and pay your money, put on the gown, and climb up on the table. It's painful—there's no getting around that. You hear this noise, sort of like when you're in the dentist's office. They went through the standard birth control line, but that was the only counseling. I didn't use birth control most of the time. I knew about it, but I didn't use it, probably just because it was a pain. It probably goes along with the old thing that I wasn't thinking.

I think I tried not to think of those pregnancies as babies. But I sure do now.

After the third abortion, things started to change. They just weren't clicking anymore. I'd go into a place I used to hang out and try to find someone to dance with, and nobody was even dancing with me. Then, too, I heard that there was something floating around that was worse than clap, that you could die from it—the beginning of the AIDS scare. I was drinking heavily, trying to drink truck drivers under the table. It just wasn't as much fun as it used to be; so I just quit, changed my lifestyle.

I started spending a lot more time at home. Then I saw

a notice at work about square dance lessons. I thought, "I'll give it a shot; maybe it will be fun." It just clicked right away. Here was a bunch of single people, just having a ball. I was dancing next to this one man one night a few weeks later, and he became my husband.

After living life in the fast lane, dating Matt was like running into a brick wall! He came from a very close family, strong values. He'd grown up a little bit slower than a lot of people do, hadn't gone out much. The first time he kissed me was at a New Year's Eve party. We'd gone out on the quiet, snow-covered lake for a walk, and there were all these millions of stars. Talk about romance! I'll never forget that night.

When we started getting serious, I laid everything on the line and told him about the abortions. He listened to what I had to say. He accepted it and forgave. He wanted to help me. That fall we got engaged, and the following summer we were married. We have a happy, successful marriage. It's definitely a blessing from God. We love each other so much.

God came back into my life after we were married. We were going to adult information classes for my husband to join my church. Some things started coming up in the classes. I stayed after to talk to the pastor, and I started crying. He spoke to me about God's grace, and that helped me a lot; but I didn't tell him about the abortions.

My faith has given me the strength to start to resolve some of these problems. I'm going to a Christian counselor now and learning about who I am and about my feelings. It's like my husband and I and God are a triangle—that's how I feel about our marriage. That's given me the love and security I need.

The most important thing I want is peace, and that's what I'm working on. It's tough, because I killed those three babies. We would just love to have a child now, but we're trying to be realistic. I'm going to have to keep working; money is so tight. I don't know if I have it in me to go to work and leave this little baby behind. I know kids need routine, and we don't have one. I'm so tired now; I wonder what I would do if I had a kid? I'd be exhausted. My eating is out of control, and I've gained a lot of weight. It just really hurts that we want a baby so bad and that we're choosing not to now. I don't know when that will change.

All these feelings keep flooding back in, about what I did to three babies I had, from my body. It just hurts so bad. Now I've got a loving and caring husband, and we have a life together, and everything is rosy, as they say. But when the feelings come back, it's so hard that sometimes I don't know what to do.

I don't know if I've forgiven myself yet. That's one of the things I still have to work through. I keep telling myself that I know that God forgave me; that's why Jesus died on the cross. But have I really forgiven myself? I don't know.

I don't know how doctors can say there are no consequences to abortion. I would like to go up to some of these doctors and show them what it really does to a person.

But the whole experience did kind of finally put me in touch with who I am. I didn't know that until a few years ago. I was finally able to wake up out of the dreamland or something that I was always in.

The only people, other than my husband, I've ever told about the abortions are two of my sisters. One of them told me about her affair, and I told her about the abortions. We just cried and hugged. The other one is very sick. She told me that she's felt a lot of loss in things that have happened over the years, and now she understands that I have too. I never told my mother. What good would it have done? She died in 1986. I haven't told my father either.

All my life I knew what I was doing was wrong; but I

needed something—the closeness of a relationship—that I never had. So I totally went the wrong way. While I was doing it I didn't feel very much. I'd just go out and have a blast. The men made me feel like I was something, even though what I was was a tramp. I really feel like a different person now. Maybe the Holy Spirit was working on me for years, and I didn't even know it—he's a lot tougher than I am.

Today I'm active in my home church again, the one from my childhood. My faith is helping me so much. It's giving me the strength to finally dry my eyes and get on with my life. At least I'm trying. I really do know that God has forgiven me. Now I just have to work on me. I'm not home yet.

JEANINE: *I'm not home yet*

**I long to dwell in your tent forever and take refuge
in the shelter of your wings. (Psalm 61:4)**

*the road is smooth
and all downhill
the road that leads
away from home*

*I never consciously set out
to leave the Father's house
I simply wandered off
to find my place in life
one day I opened up my eyes
and saw my life for what it was
the squalor and the guilt
my hunger and my shame
my loneliness and pain
far away from home*

*now how return again?
how can I go back
after everything I've done?
perhaps I could earn my way
back home again
his worthy child no more
I might hope to gain
a servant's role
within the Father's house*

*the road that led away
was all downhill
the road is lonely
dark and rough and very steep
the road that goes back home*

*I know, my child
I know your pain
how lonely it is away from home*

*how dark, how rough the road
you've walked
I've walked it too*

*I know that road, my child
I've borne your sin and walked
    your road,
the lonely road of guilt and pain
the road to shame and death
far away from home*

*"My God," I cried from that cross
of mine
"Where are you?
Why have you forsaken me?"
but no answer came
only darkness
only grief
only shame*

I know, my child

*I've cried your tears
I've died your death
at Calvary
far away from home*

*but now that's past
"Welcome home, my Son," he said
    to me
"Your death is done
the guilt is gone
my wrath is past
take up your crown again
your Easter day is come:
come home"*

you see, my child?
I know what sin can do to you
and so I see your tears
I hear your pain
I know
I really know

but now there's life
my grace is free
my love is full
my peace is real
and it's for you
come home, my child
come home

Rhonda

"What a mother is and is not . . . I have not given birth to a child, but I have been pregnant. What does that make me?"
from Rhonda's writings

Rhonda is very young, only 22. The most influential person in her life was very old, her grandmother.

Sometimes the message of God's forgiveness doesn't come through traditional channels: the church or a minister. Sometimes it comes quietly, through a person who doesn't even know he or she is being God's instrument. Rhonda's grandmother didn't know; but as she died, painfully, from cancer, she brought a message of hope, love, and forgiveness to Rhonda, forgiveness for a sin that the grandmother didn't even know existed.

What Rhonda has gone through has given her a maturity rare in one so young. Pretty, with a defiant tilt to her chin and challenge in her dark eyes, Rhonda is finally ready to let go of the past: the young man who left her and the baby she got rid of because he didn't want it. She hasn't dated in years, but she's finally ready now—ready to move on with her life.

Does her grandmother know? Perhaps. Perhaps not. But it doesn't matter. Rhonda knows.

† † † † †

I was always the talker and the entertainer in my family.

I was born in Minnesota, but later we moved to northern Wisconsin. I have three older sisters. Our family was always very close. I have cousins who are four and five times removed who are part of the family. I was always close to my grandparents and also, especially, to my father. I think he's a pretty neat guy. My mother and I used to have a few problems, but that's because we were competing for Dad! Since I moved out of the house and we each have our own territory, it's better. She's a real great lady, and we're good friends now. I guess I've always known that if I needed something I could go to my family.

Religion was always important in my family. It's been passed down and down in our lives. My grandmother read her devotion book daily all her life, 'til it got to the point that it was falling apart. She had it memorized. That's something that she passed down to us: Rather than give us her possessions, she sat down with us and talked to us about the Lord. I just couldn't have asked for anything better.

I was an average student. I didn't apply myself like I should have—I liked to look out the window and talk to people! In high school I talked even more, passed even more notes. But I was in the high B area anyway.

I started dating when I was 16. Not real serious dating, just kind of for the heck of it, a date here and a date there. I've only had one steady boyfriend in my life. That was when I had just turned 17. We went out for a little less than a year.

About the time I started dating him, I had quite a few of the normal teen-age clashes with my family. I got into that phase where nothing made me happy. I wanted my parents to be there but at the same time to just let me go about my own way. I had these ideas in my head about what a teenager was supposed to do, but, in my mind, they weren't letting me do it. If the curfew was midnight,

I'd come in at one—just testing, seeing how far I could go.

My dad wasn't one to confront that. He was a very sensitive man, and when he sat down to talk to me about it, he'd usually end up crying. He'd say, "I don't want you to end up messing up your life."

I was 17 when we became sexually active; my boyfriend was three or four years older. There was a part of me that said, "This isn't right, you shouldn't do this, your parents wouldn't want you to do this." At the same time there was a teenage part of me that was saying, "But you really love this man. He's good for you, and this is what you do when you love someone." That's what everyone tells you, so it seemed OK.

We started out using birth control, but then we stopped. He didn't want to use a condom anymore. I said, "If you're not going to, then we're not going to." But then my other side kicked in again with "But you really love him." He kept on with the "if you really love me . . ." and "we're going to be together forever so . . ." bits. So I thought, "What the heck." I was too afraid to go on the pill because I was afraid my parents would find out, and it would hurt them. The immature teenager side of me won out, and we went ahead anyway.

We went out nine or ten months before I found out I was pregnant, right before graduation. I went to the Planned Parenthood clinic in town to get the test. I was kind of shocked in a way, yet also, in a sense, happy. I've always loved children; I've always wanted children. To me the greatest thing in the world would be to give birth to a child and raise it. If I never had anything else in the world, that's the one thing I would want. My family was so great that it just seemed natural for me to bring someone else into that home. But the other side was that I was afraid that I was too young, that I would not be a good mother. What if my parents, who had been so great up to this point, decided that this was too much to handle? There was the pain for them. One of my sisters has a birth defect, spina bifida, and I wondered, "If my child had something like that, would I be able to handle it?"

I told my boyfriend. His response was to bring up the fact again of what my parents and our church would say. He sort of fed into my fears. He looked at it that I could have one or the other—him or the baby—but not both. I had to make a decision about which one I wanted. I had just turned 18 and was trying to plan what I wanted to do in the fall. He said that, if I went through with the pregnancy, I wouldn't be able to go to school, and if my parents kicked me out, he wouldn't be able to take me in.

I guess I was just so desperately looking for something to hang on to that he seemed like the best choice. He was there. I could see him. I knew he was OK, but the baby I wasn't sure about. I guess that's how I made the decision.

He offered to pay for the abortion. He and his sister went along. I was 18 so there was nothing about making me tell my parents. Looking back on it, I wish I had been 17, and they would have made me tell them, because later I found out that it would have been OK. We would have worked things out.

He went out shopping for blue jeans while I was in the clinic. The day was really long. I got there early in the morning, and it seemed like I sat there all day. I saw a counselor, who told me what it would be like, and had a blood and urine test. They gave me a couple of different pills—one made me very sleepy, and the other one made me sick. I went in for a pelvic exam to see how far along I was. I had a counselor with me during the abortion. It was painful, besides the fact that I really didn't want to do it. Even at that point I didn't. I only got through it because I thought there was someone there waiting for me, to take care of me after. I found out real quick that wasn't true.

All it would have taken is for someone who cared for me to tell me, "Don't do this." But I didn't tell the people who would have said that, my family or my best friend. I know she would have said, "Hey, you know your family is going to stick with you. Don't let him put this stuff in your head. I'm here for you, let's go tell them." But my boyfriend had told me not to tell her, so I didn't; and I went through with it.

I felt so alone. I think even the doctor sensed that, because when I left he asked if my boyfriend was with me. I said he was, and the doctor said, "When you see him, walk up to him, push him on the floor, and kick him in the stomach. Then tell him that he doesn't begin to feel what you feel." I will never forget that as long as I live.

When I told my boyfriend that, he just said, "Huh?" He kept rushing me to get going. When we got home, he dropped me off at his sister's house and said, "Let me know if anything happens," and went out on a date with someone else.

It was raining that night. I've always loved the rain, so I went out for a long walk. I had a lot of guilt feelings right away. When I made the appointment, a part of me was saying, "You are going to regret this." But there was another part of me that wanted so much to believe him that everything was going to be OK. That side tried very hard to override the guilt, but it didn't work.

I never went out with him again. I was so guilty, angry, and hurt. I swore that I'd never let anyone lie to me like that again. Over the past five years, he's tried a few times to come back, once when another girlfriend of his was pregnant and just two weeks from her due date. He wanted to get back together with me!

I continued to live at home and went to vocational school to become a secretary. I wasn't sure what I really wanted to do, and that was something I could do quickly and cheaply, until I decided. I didn't date at all. My mother says now that she suspected something was wrong, because I went through a tremendous personality change. I got to be very short, very angry—any little thing would set me off. I became withdrawn and had a great need to be in control of every situation. No matter who I was with and what we were doing, I had to be the one with the say-so. For example, even when we traveled in the car, I had to have the map, and I had to have all the directions written down. I couldn't stand to have anything go out of control. I had to stay on my own path. If I knew I couldn't control a situation or a person, I refused to get involved.

There was a lot of tension in my family. I was impossible to talk to; I made it very difficult for them. They were trying to work around something that they didn't know about. They knew I had changed, but they didn't know why. It was so hard to please me—nothing did, even if they bent over backwards. So it was very frustrating for them. They wanted to help me, but I wouldn't let them. They tried so hard, and I just told them to leave me alone.

I got a job in a small hardware company. I lived at home a little longer, and then I moved out. It was something I had to do because I knew I wasn't being fair to them. The only way I could handle it was to get out on my own, have my own space, and start doing my own thing.

I thought about the abortion quite a bit. It got to the point that just a song on the radio could put me in tears or make me such a grump that no one could talk to me. People never knew what they would say that would set me off. I started to drink quite a bit, but that didn't help. I didn't want to tell anyone what I was feeling, so I would write poetry. I remember one poem I wrote when I was thinking about telling my mother:

"Did it hurt?" she asked
With a tear in her eye.
I would like to say no,
But that would be a bigger lie.

"I cannot believe it is true!"
I wish I could say it was a mistake,
To save the pain in her eyes,
But it is too late.

"Why did you not come to me sooner?"
She wanted to help out,
That I knew was true,
But there was so much doubt.

"What did it feel like?"
That question I will not answer.
I will spare her the pain,
But the feelings begin to stir.

"I see the pain in your eyes."
No, she only sees a portion.
She does not have to live
With the memory of an abortion.

I spent so much time alone in my own place, working it
out on my own. My friends tell me that I was so calm; I
didn't show any emotion over anything.

Seven or eight months later my Mom came right out
and asked me. She tells me that I was dropping large
hints, so I guess I wanted to tell them; but I wasn't aware
of it. One day as I was packing for a trip to California, she
stopped over and she said, "Before you leave, there's one
thing I want to know. Was there a baby?"

I just about fainted, but she told me that she had suspected for a while and didn't want me to get on a plane and go somewhere without having that resolved, in case something happened to either of us.

"Yes," I answered quietly.

I give her a lot of credit. I know she wanted to fall apart, but she just said, "OK, do you want to tell me about it?"

She was angry at the guy for what he had done to me, and she was devastated that I had to go through that alone. That, more than anything, caused her hurt and pain. She thought she should have guessed it sooner. She told Dad while I was on my trip. When I got back, we sat down and talked about it. That was when they told me it would have been OK, that I could have kept the baby. I felt so sad, knowing that the one side of me was right, that it would have worked out if I had told them. I realized then that I had hurt a lot of people in doing what I had done.

I told myself that I was healed then. I told myself that things were so much better. I'd be OK for a while, but then it would all come back. I wasn't going to church very often at the time; I found lots of reasons not to go. I felt so ashamed when I walked in; I just didn't want to be there. I didn't think what I had done could be forgiven. I thought that even God could not forgive it. I was sure I was going to spend the rest of my life alone, because no one would ever want me because of what I had done.

The resolution for me didn't start until a few months ago, four years after the abortion. We found out that my grandma had cancer. In August she started to really go downhill. I was over there a lot, taking care of her. With the type of faith she had, it was hard to be around her and not have it rub off on you. Even though she didn't know about the abortion, she was constantly telling me, "Our Lord is a forgiving God. You just have to trust in him." It started sinking in to me that, yes, it was true.

Then I realized that I had to set myself free from the

ghosts I'd been living with for such a long time. My oldest sister and I had had a blowup and not talked to each other for two years. She lost her job and moved back home and started helping with grandma too. Part of my healing was burying old bones with her. We talked about what had gone wrong, and I was able to forgive her.

Then I moved on to forgiving my ex-boyfriend. I knew that, until I forgave him, I wouldn't be able to let go of him. He'd always be there, holding me back from other relationships.

My grandmother finally died in November, and that was another part, letting go of something else. She died about the time that it would have been the child's fourth birthday. It was an emotional time, and it had a big effect on me.

I went out of town the week after she died, to visit a friend, one who knew about the abortion but who I hadn't seen for a long time. It was there that I finally let it all out, I guess you could say. I don't know what finally set it off, but I threw quite a fit for about two hours—kicked and screamed and hit and said things that I'd never said to anyone: "I can't take it any more; it's more than I can handle; all this keeping it inside is driving me crazy; I can't sleep at night; I have a godchild who is four years old, and I can't enjoy her because every time I see her it drags me into a depression." My friend was quite taken aback, rather shocked! But she just stood there and let me go about my thing.

I got up the next morning feeling 50 pounds lighter. I found myself smiling in the shower; I hadn't done that for so long. I knew earlier that God had forgiven me, but I couldn't accept it because I hadn't forgiven myself. Now I could.

It wasn't that I lost my faith during those years when I struggled alone. I think I just covered it up. I was so filled with guilt that I didn't think it applied to me any more. But my grandma assured me of all that I had known, and that's what started it all for me. She never knew, but it came through her. She never knew how much she was helping me.

Today I'm still on my own. I have a good job, and I've moved into a better apartment, bought new furniture and a car. But every once in a while I still stop and say, "You've got all this, but was it worth it?" And I know it wasn't. Even though I like my life, it isn't worth what I lost. I denied myself the one thing that really would make me happy. To this day, I would like to have that child. I want a child someday, but I don't want to marry just anyone to replace what I lost years ago. I have to be careful that I don't do that.

I'm hopeful for the future now. Now I can say I think it's going to be OK. A few months ago, I couldn't have said that.

The whole experience has made me grow up, become more responsible, and realize what's really important in life. It's not the size of my paycheck or the color of my car. It's the family I have standing behind me, my friends, and God.

He's a big part of all this. There were times when I didn't think he was there, but I know now I didn't want him to be there, because I was so ashamed of what I had done. But he knew, and now I know that I can't continue to heal without him.

RHONDA: *I've always loved the rain*

You gave abundant showers, O God;
you refreshed your weary inheritance. (Psalm 68:9)

the rain came down
so silently out of the black above
the wetness cool upon my cheeks
and mingled there with burning
*   tears*
my bitter tears of pain
the rain came down
and ran in puddles on the sidewalk
sparkling softly in the streetlight
but drab within my heart
the rain came down
like endless tears from some deep
*   well of mourning*
some never ending spring of
*   sorrow welling up inside*
the rain came down

and through the rain I walked
and cried and walked some more
walked on and on
into the blackness of that night
and wept my bitter tears
falling down like rain
to settle deep within my soul
to settle there in silent pools of sorrow
and cry some more
I walked into the night and rain
weeping for the child that would
*   never be*
the child who would never walk
*   with me into the rain*
the child who would never laugh
*   and love and live*
the rain came down that night
and through the rain I walked
*   and wept*
weeping for the child I killed

the victim of my weakness and
*   my fear*
the rain came down

I learned to live once more
to work and sleep and cope
to even laugh again
but deep inside
the rain kept coming down
I walked and cried so silently
in the darkness of my private pain
and no one knew or cared
the rain came down

take heart, my child
and trust in me
I was with you on that night
the rain came down
when first you mourned the child
*   who died*
and I've been with you all the while

each tear you've shed
every tear of sorrow and of grief
I've known them all
and watched and loved
but not from far away
the rain was mine that night
falling down to weep with you
you thought you walked apart
that night the rain came down
but I was there unseen

you thought you struggled all alone
with remorse and fear and guilt

yet on that lonely battlefield
I fought for you
I was your strength and shield
that dark and lonely night
for you were not alone
you've been my child
since first I claimed you as my own
by water and the Spirit's breath
buried with me in my own death
raised up with me to live again
born anew as my own child
that water was your birth

as surely as the rains came down
to flood the earth
destroying sin yet giving life
to Noah and his family
so my washing rescued you
wiped out your sin
and brought you life
new life, my life in you

though you forgot your faith
I stayed faithful to my promise
the Spirit's seal
the mark you wore
my cross inscribed within that
    sacred font
both tomb and womb for you
the death of all your sin
the source of all your life in me

this water rich in grace
recalls your true identity
baptized in name of Father, Son,
    and Spirit
you're my dear child
I love you now as then
and shielded safe within my heart
you're never all alone

so whenever rain falls down
    again on you
remember who you are
by water and my word
remember me when rain comes down
then weep no more
forgiven, go and sin no more
in me you're free

Annalee

A rebel—that was Annalee. Deeply into the drug culture, she ran away from home at 14 and lived on the streets, sleeping under bridges and eating out of garbage dumpsters. Pregnant, she aborted her baby. Iron-hearted with pride, she wouldn't admit to her frantic parents that she needed help. She tried to do it all on her own.

God, however, can soften even the most iron-bound heart. In Annalee's case, he used a baby. She came within minutes of a second abortion, but left the clinic when something spoke to her. Today she believes it was God, and that he used her baby to "straighten her out."

Through that child, he also called her back to him. He assured her of forgiveness, and now he's given her a new calling—counselor for a pregnancy hot-line and speaker at pro-life meetings.

Because Annalee's life has been so chaotic, much of it lived in a haze of drugs and some of it blocked from memory, her story is sometimes choppy and disjointed. Yet, she has come through it all to healing. God and her loving, forgiving family worked together to accomplish that.

But that doesn't mean her pain is gone. She expressed that in a fragment of a poem she wrote a year ago:

> I lost more than my child
> In taking their advice
> I lost part of my soul
> I'll spend the rest of my life paying the price.

I know it seems abortion's the way
It's worth anything if your troubles end
But do you realize the price you must pay
Just how much are you willing to spend?

So please think, young ladies
I know now things I didn't know then
It's all over in a short time
But the pain never ends.

† † † † †

My parents were divorced when I was in first grade; they've both remarried since. I have two full sisters and a brother, and from my parents' remarriages I have five more: two half sisters from my father, and two half brothers and a sister from my mother. We're very close today, all of us. We're all one family; we don't believe in the halfs and the steps. My parents now are like best friends. I spent my childhood in a small town in Wisconsin with my mother, but when I was 13 I went to live with my father in Ohio.

The divorce affected me really bad, although I didn't realize it at the time. No one did, even my parents. It showed up in later years, when it came out that I was very angry at them.

I had some religious upbringing. We went to church and Sunday school, but it wasn't very real to me until many years later.

After I moved to Ohio, my step mother—who was my mother's best friend while my parents were married—and I didn't get along at all (although today we are practically best friends). My father was gone all the time, so even though I went to live with him, I really ended up living with her.

I had a real hard time in school. I was a kid going

through a lot of problems, the peer pressures and other things. I did a great deal of drinking and drugs. Every type of drug you can think of, I've done. I got quite heavily into LSD and speed. I've always been a person who didn't like to be alone and when I had the drugs, I didn't care if I had anybody or not.

I lost my virginity when I was 14. Ironically, I was the last one of my friends—everyone else did by 12 or 13. Kids really pressure you when you are the last one to do anything. I was in the ninth grade and it was hard. I thought, "I might as well, just to be like everyone else."

I ran away from my father and stepmother's when I was 14 and was gone for a month and a half. Then I got caught and sent back to Wisconsin to live with my mother, but I was too much for her to handle. She finally said, "You can go back to Ohio or do whatever you want."

I was just such a rebellious kid, and my parents couldn't put up with it (now as an adult I realize that I wouldn't have put up with it either!). I didn't want anyone telling me what to do or how to do it; I wanted to be on my own. My parents gave me the choice to either straighten up or get out. I got out.

I know I hurt my parents badly. I realize now that they were not giving up on me. They just couldn't handle it anymore. I had younger brothers and sisters who were seeing what I was doing and looking up at me as the cool one, and my parents had to think about them too.

I moved out of the house. At first I stayed at a hotel. A friend of mine paid for it. He was the person I got my drugs from, and it gave him and his friends a place to party. I was right across the street from the police station while the police from Ohio and Wisconsin were all looking for me!

Then I moved in with a friend and her mother. The mother helped me a lot, but once she started telling me that I had to get a job or I had to do this or that—I was gone.

I lived on the streets for a whole year, slept on the beach. That's where everyone hung out. That's where I'd be all day anyway, so at night I'd just go under the docks. I could take showers there and wash clothes. I had a little beach bag with my toothbrush and stuff. When you are living on the streets you hide things in different places, wherever you sleep, so I had stuff stashed here and there.

Keeping clean is the biggest problem—you don't stay too clean, but you really don't care. Once I pried open a machine in a rest room that had a cloth towel and cut it up to make towels and washcloths. It was hard when I had my period—I'd use toilet paper or paper towels from rest rooms. Friends would lend me clothes. A few nights, when it got cold, I stayed with friends and could get cleaned up there. But you really don't think of yourself as being scummy. You're 16; you're on your own; you're cool.

To eat, I'd hang around the mall, and when people would throw away half-eaten food, I'd go take it. It sounds disgusting I know, but when you're on the streets you do anything you must to survive. I'm 5' 11", and at one time I was down to 94 pounds; but you just do the best you can.

I had the same boyfriend that whole year. He was seven years older than me. He had a job and an apartment. Sometimes I would stay with him, but as strange as it sounds, he didn't know I wasn't living anywhere. I just told him I didn't have a phone and didn't want him to come over.

I took drugs the whole time, but I never sold them. You know, people think you need money to get drugs, but you don't. If you have friends, they'll give you some of theirs. Especially young girls. It's sad, but that's what people do. They figure that if they give drugs to someone with no money, she'll tell her friends, and they'll all come and buy.

A lot of drug dealers get new clients by giving drugs to young kids, and they go tell their older brothers and sisters. So either way, the dealers make money.

I was pretty young, but living on the streets makes you grow up a lot faster. I dropped out of high school, so I don't have the diplomas and stuff, but I have a lot of knowledge you can't get from going to school. I remember one night when a drunk tried to attack me when I was sleeping on the beach. He had a knife, and I had to run for my life. You learn. I know now that I can get through anything. I have no doubts that, whatever I face in life, I can get through it.

To tell the truth, I hated living on the streets, but I had so much pride that I would not go back to my parents. I would not ask for their help. One night I slept outside my father's garage; but when he came out in the morning, I hid because I didn't want them to know I wasn't making it. Kids who run away often get in so deep that they don't know how to turn around and come home. My parents didn't know if I was alive or dead.

After a year on the streets, I moved in with a friend's mother again. While I was living with her, I got pregnant. I never told my boyfriend. The woman's older son took me to get a pregnancy test, took me for the abortion, and lent me the money. I didn't think much about it; it was cut and dried. I thought there was no way I could have had a child then.

I had no counseling at that clinic. There were no options offered to me. They didn't ask my age (I was only 16). They didn't ask how I got the money. They just told me what they were going to do. There was no cover on the tank during the abortion, so I saw the whole thing. Then I laid down for an hour. They gave me a cookie and a glass of juice and told me to go on my way. I really don't remember how I felt, I think I blocked much of it out. I just kept telling myself it was the best thing to do. I didn't think about how my parents would feel, that the baby inside of me was their grandchild. I didn't think of my brothers and sisters, that it was their niece or nephew. I only thought about myself. I had it done and went on my way.

About three months later, I broke up with my boyfriend and got involved with a man who was heavily into dealing drugs. His life was in danger because of a disagreement over a drug deal, and he wanted me to leave because he was afraid I'd get hurt too. He asked me where I wanted to go, and I said Vermont, because that's where my best friend had moved. Within an hour I was on a plane; none of my friends even knew where I had gone.

I met a man there, Earl, who is now my husband, and I got pregnant again. He broke up with me an hour before I found out I was pregnant.

I tried to abort myself by using too much cocaine, enough that I thought any baby would die. But I didn't have a miscarriage, so I went to have another abortion. Earl gave me the money. I was all the way in the room, on the table, when I said, "I can't do this. I can't go through it again." Something in my head told me that this wasn't right, and I got up and left.

I called my mother—that was the only thing I could think of to do at the time. I hadn't talked to her in a year, but the first thing she said to me was, "How are you?"

"I'm four months pregnant."

"Come home," she said.

She sent me a plane ticket, and when I got home, she had an apartment rented and all furnished for me.

I had planned to give this baby up for adoption, but my daughter was born six weeks early, and she had heart problems. I went through a lot of guilt because I was sure it was the cocaine that caused her problems, although the doctor says there's no way to know for sure. I also had been very malnourished before I came home.

I went home to my mother's, and the baby stayed in the hospital because she only weighed four pounds. I was going through a living hell, trying to decide if I was doing the right thing by giving her up. I was never very religious, but at that point I said to my mother, "I keep asking God to give me an answer, and he's not telling me anything."

At that moment the phone rang, and it was the hospital. They said the baby had to have immediate heart surgery or she would die, and I was the only one who could sign the form, because I was her mother. Right then and there I decided that I was keeping my child. There were no doubts about it. I named her Carrie.

She had her surgery. The first time I held her, she had tubes coming out of her everywhere. I still felt a lot of guilt that maybe I had done that to her, but she survived and did well after the surgery.

She had severe health problems later though—spinal meningitis when she was six months, seizures when she was a year. For a while I really lost all sense of faith in God, because the doctors kept telling me she wasn't going to make it; and I thought it was God getting even with me for all I've done. But then I realized that it was God who was getting her through all this. Now I really believe that God gave me Carrie to straighten me out, because after I came back here and had her, I never did drugs again.

I've changed so much; I'm a completely different person now. A lot of it was because of her. I realized that she is a real human being; she's not going to just go away. I decided that I don't want her to live like I did. I want her to know that I love her, and I want her to look at me and be proud of her mother, not see someone who is drinking and doing drugs. I really believe that, if it weren't for Carrie, I would be dead right now. I would have either

died of an overdose, or something else would have happened to me. I was so self-destructive. I think she helped
me realize that I had to get my life in order, if not for me,
then for her.

When Carrie was two, I took her back to Vermont to see
her father. We began rebuilding our relationship and soon
became engaged. He had been into a great deal of drugs
back there, but once we were engaged he moved back to
Wisconsin with me, and he got off drugs too.

We got married three years ago, and things are going
fantastically. We are happy, and we've just bought a house.
Earl's been a tremendous help to me. He told me right
before we got married that I was going to get off welfare,
that we were going to make it on our own. And we have. I
got certified as a nurses' aide and started working in a
nursing home. I soon realized that this is the life for me.

I had blocked the abortion out and hadn't told anyone
about it, but while we were engaged I told Earl. He said he
really wasn't surprised, considering the life I led. Many
girls who are homeless end up pregnant because they turn
to sex to get a place to stay. And prostitution. I was
approached many times by pimps because I was a young
girl on my own, and they knew that; but I never did prostitution. I think it was because I did have some religious
upbringing. That was one thing that I always knew deep in
my gut was wrong. It was still my body, and I wasn't going
to throw it to just anybody. I had sex, but it was always in a
long-term relationship. It was never just a one-time thing.

I was very lucky with my parents. My mother has a fan-
tastic philosophy that a parent's love is unconditional. She
tried to reach out to me many times, but I just pushed her
away. She welcomed me back; she and my older sister
were wonderful. They forgave me for many things. They
took care of me while I was pregnant—taking me to doctor appointments and making sure I was eating. When I

was considering giving the baby up for adoption, they all said, "We'll stand behind you, whatever you decide to do. We love you, and we want you to do whatever is best."

Then when I decided to keep Carrie, everyone in my family came and said, "This is what we wanted you to do." They all helped me with clothes and stuff for Carrie.

They told me they loved me, and slowly I regained their trust. It took a long time for me to learn how to tell people how I feel, but now I'm the type of person who is always hugging and touching and saying, "I love you." I think a lot of kids lack hearing that. Even though my family was close, we didn't *hear* "I love you" a lot, and I think I needed to hear it.

My father and I are very close now too. I held it against him for a long time: it was his fault I lived on the streets; it was his fault I had so many problems, because he was gone all the time. But I know now that's not true.

I don't blame my family for anything that happened to me, because they tried, they really tried hard to help me. I brought it all on myself. I take complete blame.

God came into my life after I had Carrie. My mother's children all go to church and to a church school. I would look at them, and look back at how I was when I was on the streets, and I could see that those kids have morals and values, something I didn't have. I wanted my daughter raised in that too, so I started going to church with them. I decided to go through the private membership class, even though I didn't think I would believe it, just so my daughter could go to the school. Once I started going, I realized that this was something I needed in my life.

When we got to the fifth commandment and started talking about abortion, I just lost it. I started sobbing; I didn't even know why. The pastor asked me what was wrong and suddenly the whole thing came out. He said, "Annalee, the Lord has forgiven you, I think it's about time you forgive yourself." It hit me that I was at that class for a reason—God knew that I needed to know I was forgiven.

My daughter is now six years old, and I see such faith in her. My grandmother, who I was really close to, just died, and Carrie said, "Mommy, Grandma's with God, and some day we'll go to see her again." For a six-year-old to have so much faith that it can get her through something like that—it's wonderful. And besides all that, I just found out I'm pregnant again.

I felt a strong need to help women, so I've started working with a church-sponsored pro-life group. I don't want other women to go through this like I did. I don't want girls to go into it blindly like I did. I wasn't told that I was going to have these feelings of grief, like I lost a child, that whenever I looked at a child I would think of that baby, that it isn't something you just forget.

Last week was the first time I ever talked in front of a whole group, when I told my story at a group meeting. I didn't think I was going to get through it, I was crying so hard. It was rough. My mother and my younger brother were in the audience, and that helped a lot.

After I left I felt such a sense of relief. This is going to sound strange; but I felt, while I was talking, like the soul of that baby was looking down on me and saying, "Now you've accomplished it." I felt like maybe God had a reason for me, to be able to help others. I've signed up to take the training to become a counselor on their hot-line.

I want to tell women that the pain from an abortion never ends. I look at my daughter now and think about what a beautiful child she is and how much she has given to my life, and I can't believe how close I came to killing her. I think about the new baby and wonder if that other baby would have been a boy or a girl, what it would look like now. I really believe that you can block those feelings out for a long time, but you are going to have to deal with them some day.

It's sad because women who lose a child, say in still-birth, can grieve, and they get over it. But for women who've had an abortion, you grieve your lost child, but society doesn't stand behind you. They don't have any support, nowhere to go. That's a horrible thing to live with. Most mistakes you can turn around and change somehow, but this one you can't.

Looking back over my life, this sounds strange, but I'd do it, except for the abortion, the same way all over again. I had it hard, but I realize now that experience has helped me appreciate what I do have. It helped me realize that there are people out there who need help. There are places you can go for help; but when you're on the streets, you don't know about those places.

That's why I want to help. I want to work one-on-one with women, and I want to do more speaking to groups. I want to tell women what it feels like after. I've lost a child. I've lost part of my soul that I will never be able to get back. If I can help even one girl to not have an abortion, then there will be a reason for the baby I sacrificed.

ANNALEE: *the pain never ends*

**For I know my transgressions, and my sin is always before me.
(Psalm 51:3)**

*it seemed so clear
a carefree life
no hassles, no entanglements
no complicated conversations
nothing left to do except to be
just sand and sun and me
it seemed so clear*

*the nights were cold
the daytimes lonely
lots of people everywhere
but few who knew or cared
about my loneliness and pain
it was clear to me
much too clear for me*

*one truth grew ever larger:
feelings set you up for failure
a helpless pawn in the game called
   life
feelings leave you naked and
   exposed
vulnerable defenseless victim
in a power-hungry world
feelings are a liability*

*and so I dulled the pain
covered up the clarity
found relief and solace
in capsules and syringes
my great big wooden numbness
that passed for peace
but wore off into pain*

*I looked for love
but hid from those who really
   loved me*

*my carefree days of sun and sand
grew dark and overcast
my endless search for peace
of mind and heart and soul
led as far as body only
I took comfort where I found it
in touch of skin
and bodies wrapped together
it felt like love to me*

*nothing seemed clear any longer
except the pain and hurt
and so I hid myself each place I could
in laughter
in drugs
in men
they were all the same to me
anything would do
any price I'd pay
in order not to feel
to cover up and hide
peace at any cost was all I wanted*

*I paid in blood
my baby's blood and mine
combined inside that tank
a costly ransom price
yet still there was no peace*

*I can cover up my feelings
but there's no escaping guilt
one reality stands starkly ever clearer
though life has changed for better
my pain will never end*

hush my child and listen now:
your pain will have its end
where death shall be no more
where mourning, sighing, weeping
    cease
where tears are wiped away
by my own hand

there joy awaits
eternal joys at that great feast
the nuptials of the Lamb
the marriage bliss of the King of
    kings
and his royal bride, the church

from heaven high he stooped
    down low
to enter here and rescue her
with his own body and his blood
the pricetag of her sin
his cross-shaped death her ransom
    price
his love her life and hope

her kingly groom came with virile love
to cleanse his tarnished bride
and claim her as his own
washed clean by water and the word
unblemished, pure, and undefiled

now lift your head my child
from bitter shame and deep remorse
for though your eyes be clouded here
dark memories out of your ugly past
my eyes are clear to see you as you are

the royal table stands prepared
no need to wait for heaven's joy
to taste his love
come dine with him
and feed on him
his body and his blood
your life and hope and purity

and in this feast see clearly now:
he, the royal groom
and
you, his worthy bride

Melanie

Melanie has had one abortion, and she's a single mother, alone and pregnant again. She knows she's done some things that are not right in God's eyes, but she also knows he has forgiven her.

Melanie lives in a small farming community and belongs to a tiny church—a setting many people would not think to be supportive to a single, pregnant woman. Yet, it's through the love and support of her minister and the people in her church that Melanie has found the strength to rebuild her life.

Melanie's cold and distant family and her constant battle with being overweight saddled her with a low self-image and the feeling that no one would ever love her. She escaped into relationships with two abusive husbands—"real creeps" she calls them now. However, because she felt she deserved whatever they did to her, she stayed with them until her life was literally threatened.

She still suffers from a lack of confidence, but with God providing her stability and her son and the baby-to-be to live for, she's making progress.

† † † † †

My mother says she married a sensitive, healthy, robust young man; but during World War II, he was shot in the back of the heart and left for dead. When the Red Cross came to get bodies, they found he was alive. A surgeon in a tent hospital miraculously removed the bullet and parts of his ribs, and after six months of hospital stays, he came home, weak, bitter, and sad. He had horrid nightmares, and still does at age 72. Sounds, TV shows, anniversary dates can all be triggers for him. Today we'd call it post-traumatic stress disorder, but when I was growing up all we heard was, "Don't get Dad mad, don't get him upset."

I guess he and my mother were close—at least as close as Scandinavians can be! There wasn't a lot of talking in their relationship. There still isn't, but they get along. I remember my father putting his arm around my mother once, but that's all.

I grew up on a dairy farm in the northern part of the country. Most of the time I felt unhappy; there was nobody to talk to. My sister was 14 years older than me, my brother six years older. My sister is quiet; she always tried to please my parents. I wasn't like that. I was always curious. I was the snoopy one, constantly asking questions, while she sat quietly with her hands in her lap. There was a lot of comparison—"your sister never did anything like that."

My parents never said they loved me. Never. I really don't think they did. I was just there. I think it troubled me as a child; I do remember feeling lonely a lot. The older I got, the more the distance grew between us.

On the farm we were very isolated. My parents never went anywhere. I only remember them taking one Saturday night off in 35 years. I loved school because there were other people there. Even if I didn't talk to them, I liked the activity, watching them, being around them. I was a good student. I made all A's and B's, but I never studied. My goal was to never take home a book, and I made it.

My religious upbringing was rigid. We went to church every Sunday, but it was something I did because that's what we did. It didn't mean anything.

In high school I had friends, but I wasn't allowed to go

out anywhere. In my junior year I wanted more freedom. I didn't demand it; I just took it. At first I'd tell my parents I was going out and I had a ride. That didn't go over too good, so I started sneaking around. I'm not even sure how I did it, but I did. I was supposed to be somewhere else, and I was really sneaking around with some really inappropriate guys. I started drinking on the sly. I had a boyfriend who was 25 when I was 16—at the time I thought it was cool. He had a job and a car and money. He may have been older, but he wasn't wiser. I became sexually active with him.

I think I got into sex from a need to be loved. I thought I'd have somebody of my own that would love me, and then I'd get away from home. Also, sex was the thing to do. Everybody was having sex, all my friends. Out of my six closest friends, only one didn't, and she was very religious. For me there wasn't a lot of conflict with religion, I just didn't care about it. There was just so much pressure—if you hadn't had sex, what was wrong with you?

I didn't use any birth control because my boyfriend said, "Don't worry, I've never gotten anyone pregnant before," and it wasn't available to me. There was no clinic; it wasn't taught about at school.

After graduation I wanted to go to college as my sister and brother had, but my parents said no. "You're always so wild," was what they said. I didn't think I was, but they did. They also said we didn't have enough money, and they refused to fill out the financial aid forms. We had always lived like paupers. What I wore to school was pretty embarrassing because they wouldn't buy me any clothes. Years later I found out that they wouldn't send in the financial aid forms because they knew they made too much money, and I wouldn't have qualified for any aid.

So I got a job in a meat packing plant. It was the pits of a place to work. People around here look down on people who work there, but actually, although the work is very hard, the pay is good. I worked in evisceration, so it was all blood and guts. I lived at home because I wanted to save money to go to school, but never did go because I was too busy buying clothes and a car. I'd go into town on Friday night, and I was finally having fun. I'd turned 18, and my parents couldn't tell me what to do.

I didn't have any trouble getting dates and was told I was attractive to men, even though I was overweight, but I didn't think so. I think I had a really poor self-image. I don't know what it was, but I sure got involved with some creeps. I'd always seem to find somebody with low self-esteem too, and we'd kind of feed on each other, complaining about this and complaining about that. I was sexually active with many of them, though I had periods when I wasn't at all. I think my parents suspected it, but they never said anything. We were pretty much like strangers living in the same house.

Then I got involved with the assistant supervisor at work. He had a girlfriend that he'd had three children with, but she had left him. We were working together every day and really enjoying it. The third time we went out, bang, we had sex and I got pregnant, just like that.

At first when I missed my period, I just denied it. Then I started getting sick every morning at work. When I told the man, he said, "Oh. Well, my girlfriend came back, and we just moved in together."

I couldn't turn to my parents. No way. When I was about two months along, I moved out of my parents' home. They totally objected, but I just packed and left. I moved to another town about 35 miles away, into a friend's apartment. I'd been laid off at work and was on unemployment. I didn't do much. I thought a lot about the baby. I knew I didn't want it. Well, it wasn't so much that I didn't want the baby, but I didn't know what to do with it. The father didn't want any part of it, and I thought I knew what my family would do. My brother had eloped a few years before, and my parents didn't speak to him for two years, so I figured I'd really be tossed out on my ear. I just walked around, and it was like I was watching myself, my feelings were so detached.

When I finally decided on the abortion, I had some friends who were going into the city drop me off at the clinic. I know I had to watch a film, but I don't remember any of it. They asked if I was sure I wanted an abortion. I remember the woman's face who was telling me everything, but I don't remember much what she said. I know she asked if I was scared and if I was going to regret this, and I said, "Yes, I'm scared, and yes, I'm going to regret it; but I'm going to do it anyway." And I did.

I remember the sound of when it was happening. It was just horrible, that vacuum sound. It was very painful. When it was over, the doctor said, "You must have been more than nine weeks along." I remember lying in the recovery room and feeling just sick. While I was waiting, another girl said to me, "You look so pale. This must be your first time." I told her it was my first and last. She said, "Oh, it's not so bad. This is my fifth. It gets easier."

But I told myself I'd never, ever get into this predicament again. I was really disgusted with myself. I knew I had done something horrible and was afraid I was never going to be able to forgive myself for it. I felt like a . . . murderer.

Two weeks later I went for a checkup because the terrible cramping and heavy bleeding hadn't stopped. The doctor told me I had been much too far along for a suction abortion and that it was really unsafe. He gave me pain medication, and I took it for six weeks because the cramping lasted that long.

The father's comment afterwards was, "I guess it was good for me and good for you that you had this done, but I guess it wasn't so good for the baby." I thought, "If you'd only given me one ounce of support, I wouldn't have done this." So then I had someone to hate, and that helped. After I went back to work, I would do little things to spite him. It was very immature, but I was just acting out my anger at the whole thing.

I managed to put my feelings about the abortion to the side during the day. I could picture the procedure, but I wasn't really there. But when I was asleep I had nightmares about it. I'd be there, and I'd feel the pain. I'd hear the sounds. I'd hear a baby crying, and I could see the fetus curled up in a ball. I'd wake up just sweating, feeling cold, but sweating.

Then a man I was dating introduced me to the world of marijuana. I could sleep when I smoked pot. I drank too, and they covered the pain.

I married that man. That's when I started being physically abused. He drank and did every drug he could find. I was the one who worked and took care of him. The marriage lasted about a year, during which he beat me up at least once a week. I was knocked unconscious once; I had a broken rib. He'd come home drunk at three in the morning and drag me up to have sex and cook him supper. The sex was very, very rough, but I didn't want to admit to anyone that there was anything wrong, so I stayed and covered up. He was always so remorseful the next day that I felt sorry for him. I even went to the battered women's shelter several times, but I always went back.

Finally I got so sick of it, one morning as I was cutting an orange in half, I remember thinking, "I'm already a murderer; I've already taken one life; what does it matter?" I went into the bedroom with the knife in my hand and came about two feet from killing him. Then I backed out of the bedroom and packed. I moved back home. A few nights later he killed a man in a bar, and eventually he went to jail.

I went right into another relationship and married a man who was also an alcoholic and abusive, but the abuse was different. It wasn't predictable; I never knew when it was going to happen. I got pregnant with my son, and that was wonderful. I was so happy; but then I realized that, since I had a child, I had a responsibility to him, so when my son was 14 months old I left that husband. He killed himself a few months later.

I know I had a pattern of choosing unstable men. I think the abortion really lowered my self-esteem to the point where I didn't care about myself. I felt so much guilt over the abortion; I felt like I deserved whatever happened.

During the years of my marriages, I had continued to go to church, but it was entirely superficial. I don't think I really had any faith, but that changed after I left my second husband. I moved back with my parents and started going to my old church, the one I had grown up in. I went to see the pastor and suddenly found myself pouring out everything that had happened, for years back. That pastor assured me that I was forgiven, for everything, even for the abortion. At that point some of the guilt began to leave— although it was still difficult and will always be.

It's been years now, and sometimes something will be bothering me, and I don't even know what it is. Then I'll look at the calendar and realize it's close to the day I had the abortion—January 9th. I still get depressed during the first part of January, every year.

I met another man after my second husband died. He was warm and supportive and encouraging, and I was alone and vulnerable. We did have sex. He sort of hooked me into it because he just wanted a sort of free-and-easy thing, and I'm pregnant now. But we are not going to get married. It troubles me a lot that I'm pregnant outside of marriage. There isn't a day that goes by that I don't wake up terribly upset by it. For half a day I thought about another abortion—there was my answer, quick and easy. But then I realized I couldn't go through with it again. No. Never! It would just be compounding the problem.

I went to my pastor and told him that I'm pregnant and I'm really scared. He told me to take a look at my son and what a good job I'm doing with him, and I knew then I would keep this baby. The father is going to take some financial responsibility.

I'm not afraid to accept help. There are support services available, and you bet I'm taking advantage of them. My pastor has been very supportive, still assuring me that I am forgiven.

I've pretty much worked through my guilt. The nightmares are gone. I can still remember them, but I know they're not real. I would have to say that the abortion caused me great distress, to the point that I felt suicidal at times, but I don't feel that way anymore.

At this point my goals are to witness my faith to my children and communicate openly with them. I want to do more than just go to church on Sunday, to make use of it. Church isn't just a building. It's a place where you can go and feel safe, and develop a relationship with other people, be yourself, and not have to pretend that you're such a good person.

I've learned that God doesn't punish people. I think I grew up thinking that if you were good, God would bring rain when you need it; but if you weren't good, he'd send a flood, and you'd drown in it. I know now that God doesn't operate that way. He is my stability, my consistency. I'd fall apart if I didn't have that. I've strayed over the line many, many times, but he doesn't punish me.

Today is the first time I felt the baby kick—and I found myself feeling that it's a gift from God.

MELANIE: *I didn't care about myself*

**My wounds fester and are loathsome
because of my sinful folly.** (Psalm 38:5)

*ugly and alone
I've lived my life
apart
I looked for love
and found pain instead
I looked for warmth
someone to care
and hold me close
someone to soothe
the ache
to heal the wound inside
but instead I found
more hurt
more ugly pain*

*I didn't care, you see
I didn't care about myself
for anyone who throws away
    a child
should be thrown away as well,
    I thought*

that was me: a throw-away

*and who could love
a throw-away?
who would care for me
when I didn't care about myself?
I loathed myself
so ugly and alone
I lived all by myself
in misery and guilt*

*would you still love me
if I told you what I've done?
would you still want to love me
if I told you who I am?*

*I know who you are, my child
I know where you've been
and what you've done
I know it all*

*I see your hurt and pain
I see, deeper still, your guilt
the ugliness of sin and shame
I see it all*

*but that's not all I see
for in my love
I've sent my Son
to take your guilt
and bear it all away*

*I see his blood
and not your sin
you're pure and clean to me
your sin erased
your guilt wiped out*

*you have my love
you have my hope
you have my life and healing
passed on to you
in washing, word, and meal*

*alone?
no more
you have my church—your family
with them it's safe to be yourself:
a sinner—loosed from sin
to live again
in hope and joy and peace*

ugly and despised?
no more
beauty is in the beholder's eye,
you see
and you're beheld by me

Penney

"Looking at me now, no one would guess about the scars that festered on my heart and soul. Christ has truly healed my scars."

Those are Penney's words. Raised in a severely dysfunctional home with an alcoholic father, who left when she was only four and left again by dying when she was 11, and a bitter, hostile mother, who saw in Penney everything she both loved and hated in her ex-husband, Penney wanted only one thing: security.

She found it by moving in with a man. She didn't love him at the time. She admits that, but he gave her strength and stability. When she became pregnant, however, that strength and stability vanished. Then he wanted nothing but to be rid of the "problem."

The solution to the problem was not without its price. "I didn't know I was going through the grieving process until somebody told me I was," Penney says. "I thought I was going crazy."

But she wasn't. Once she was able to see God's love and to know that he had forgiven her, she was able to find peace.

Today, after ten years of marriage to the father of her aborted baby and the birth of two sons, Penney says she and her husband love each other now. They have learned.

Close again to her God, who is also nudging at her husband, Penney looks forward to the future with hope. Her ultimate goal is to become a counselor, to point women suffering the aftereffects of abortion to the only place where there is hope and healing: the cross.

I grew up on the West Coast, in the state of Washington. My parents were divorced when I was four years old. I have a brother who is my mother's son, born before she married my father. I found out just recently that I also have a sister from my father and mother before they were married, who was placed for adoption (my dad couldn't get away from his former wife. In other words my mother was having a relationship with a married man and got pregnant). My father had been married several times before and had other children that I have met a few times, but I don't know them.

My brother and I have not had a good relationship over the years, because when we were younger, he thought that my father was his father. When he found out he wasn't, for some reason, he blamed me and took it out on me.

We belonged to a church. My mom started us in Sunday school before the divorce, and after my dad left, the pastor came to visit. Then my mom started going to church. I went to church school and was even confirmed.

I have no bitterness toward my father. I loved him dearly and have good memories of him, but he was an alcoholic and very much a womanizer. His inability to stay with one woman caused the divorce. There was another woman, and he left my mom. She had no desire for this to happen. I think it's true that divorce has long-lasting effects on children. As far as the immediate trauma, to be honest, the first couple of years I don't remember. I've blocked that time out; but yes, it was traumatic. There were many times when I had a difficult time dealing with the whole situation.

When I was eleven, my father died of lung and brain

cancer and heart disease. He became ill right after the divorce, and for the last three years of his life, I knew he was going to die. I saw him often up until the end, when it was difficult to see him because he was so ill; but I still saw him every month or two.

I've never seen myself as having gone through a lot. You just do it; it's the set of circumstances you live under.

My relationship with my mother was really difficult. It's taken me 20 years to come to terms with that relationship and to forgive her. I was bitter because after the divorce she became very hostile and distant from me. I've come to find out in recent years that much of her anger came because, whenever she looked at me, she would see my dad, and she never stopped loving him. To this day she still loves him. When she would look at me, it would bring back hosts of bad memories about him and the child she gave up for adoption. There was no physical abuse, but a lot of distancing. Sometimes it was a "You aren't even there" kind of attitude. It was tough. I remember the day after my father died. She callously told me that, since my brother had a hard time dealing with his feelings, he was going to stay home from school the next day; but since I had no problems, she wanted me to go. To an 11 year old child that's the same as saying, "I don't care how you feel."

From there we progressed into a very distant relation-ship. My mom has her own set of problems, serious depressions in which she has tried to take her own life. It wasn't easy for her either.

Basically, my mom was pretty straightforward, maybe too straightforward, in dealing with any issue, and that included sex. "I don't want you to do it, but if you're going to do it, be careful" was the long and the short of anything that she said. At that point we were not communicating.

I remember one encounter in my life when I was about 12 or 13 and I was playing by myself in a deserted schoolyard. This guy drove up. As I look back now I can't believe this happened, but he was naked from the waist down. He opened the car door and wanted me to come closer. I ran away, and he followed me in the car. I did get away, but my gut feeling was, "Don't tell Mom because she won't understand, she won't let you go out of the house again." I look back now and realize I could have lost my life, but the only thing I could think of then was, "she won't understand."

I would characterize myself as unhappy all during my childhood. I was very lonely. Extremely lonely. I didn't have many friends. I was overweight and definitely at the bottom of the cast. I was pretty much an above average student, but my high-strung brother was very, very intelligent with a photographic memory. My mom's thing was to always say, "You're not as smart as your brother is," so I was basically allowed to let my grades be as they were.

At one point I did have a relationship with God; there was faith there. My mother was very dependent on the pastor at our church, however. Basically, when my father left, she shifted her dependency to the pastor, but then he left. A new pastor came in, and she didn't like him, so right after I was confirmed, she left the church. She told me that if I wanted to keep on going, that was up to me. Well, that was just a few months after my father died, and, given the atmosphere at home and the things that were going on, it was natural for me to fall away too.

It was always my intent to go back; it was always in the back of my mind. I know the Lord was always with me, even during the times that I didn't necessarily want him there!

When I went to high school, I did manage to gain a little more acceptance because of some talents that I had. I had a few friends, but it wasn't spectacular. I didn't date at all until I was a senior and really didn't start socializing with men until right after high school.

Ten months after high school graduation I met Bart, the man who is now my husband. I met him through some friends—we were both involved with the basic drug crowd at that time. I had experimented with drugs in high school, but I didn't get heavily involved until right after school. I used mostly marijuana. I experimented with other things; but they were never a part of my life, and I was smart enough to stay away from the hard core stuff. I knew to stay away from things that were addictive and could ruin your life. Little did I know then that they can all ruin your life!

We were both into the drug scene, but Bart was even more so. That buried me even deeper into it. At first, drug use was just a casual thing for me, but when I met Bart, it became more of a consistent thing.

Shortly after we met, I moved in with him. At that point I wasn't looking for love, I was looking for security and looking to stop being lonely. We had to learn later to love each other, because there never was that in the first place.

My mother didn't like it that I moved in with him, but she and I weren't speaking to each other at the time. For a period of several years, our relationship was basically nonexistent. I remember that, starting right after my father left, my mother would not speak directly to me. If I talked to her, she would turn to my brother and tell him to tell me something. That was the norm for nine years. I was very bitter, very angry. Once I moved in with Bart, I felt I didn't need to even deal with that part of my life anymore.

The abortion happened shortly after I moved in with Bart. I had become sexually active when I was 18, about five months before I met him. There were three other guys, but none of those relationships lasted. They were just one-night stands. When I found out I was pregnant, I knew I couldn't begin to turn to my mother. I would have gotten one big "I told you so."

Bart had been married before and had been divorced for two years. He had a daughter and didn't want any more children then. He was very short in telling me so: made it clear to me that, if I wanted to stay with him, I would need to have an abortion. I didn't really want to have it, but I felt at that time that I didn't have a choice. I couldn't go to my parents. I couldn't stay with him. So where does a pregnant 18-year-old go?

One of the biggest things in my life at that time was finding a man who would stay with me. Security—that was a word that didn't exist to me. I had found it with Bart, so when he told me that I had a choice, for me there was no choice. Now that I had found someone who was willing to be with me, who wanted me to stay with him, I couldn't let go of that. There have been times in my life that I blamed it on him and said, "It's your fault." But I know now that it wasn't. I had a choice and I made it.

On that day, I wanted to change my mind, but I couldn't. When I got to the clinic, I wanted to say no, but I couldn't, so I went ahead and did it. The procedure hurt a little bit, but not bad at all. I remember coming out of there and crying—suddenly the tears began coming.

Bart and I had an argument afterward because he wanted to go away, motorcycle riding, that weekend. To him the abortion was just a minor surgical procedure. I remember being hurt and bitter about that. To me it was so much more, but he had no concept of that.

I felt like I was just falling apart. Some of that time right after is really foggy for me; but I remember thinking I was turning my back on everything I had learned as a child growing up, my faith, Christianity. There was never any doubt in my mind that what I had done was wrong. I always knew that it was not right. Bart left for the weekend, and it was then that I went numb.

I just went cold, blocked it all out like it didn't matter to me. But you could see in my outward life that it did. My life went into upheaval. I had a lot of difficulties with my job. I ended up quitting and for a long time didn't work at all. I couldn't seem to get anything accomplished. I went into the drugs quite a bit more than I had been. I call the next years the "seven black years of my life": numb the mind; don't feel anything. Still, the depression was definitely there.

At that point I would characterize myself as an unbeliever, yet I still prayed from time to time. I still thought about my faith. There were times when I wished I could go back to it, but I felt like I couldn't. The flame was definitely very much dampened.

A year and a half later I got pregnant again, and Bart and I got married. During my pregnancies, I only used marijuana, and, thank God, there haven't been any effects on my children. After the baby was born, in some ways it was better; but in other ways it was worse. My relationship with my husband was rocky—always uncertainty, always the arguments and fights. But there was still some security for me with him, and, because of the baby, I felt loved and wanted and important to someone. But the drug use didn't really change. Neither did the depression.

I even got to the point where I thought, to justify my own actions, that abortion should be a personal choice. I did a lot of justifying to keep from having to deal with my guilt. That guilt kept me from approaching the Lord, and I knew it. I felt that I was unredeemable, that I had dirtied myself so much in that one single act of abortion that he would never want me back. That was the biggest fear, the one thing that was persistent through those seven years. It was pretty scary.

Three years after I had my first child, I had my second, another boy. About that same time my mother went into a major depression. She was hospitalized for several weeks, and when she got out she proceeded to overdose on her antidepressants. I was the one who found her. I was very resentful of her and of my brother, because he basically didn't want to deal with her illness and just left it all up to me. I felt I had to do my best to uphold my responsibilities to her; I couldn't just let her die.

I reached a point that I was questioning everything—everything that I'd been taught, whether there even was a God. I wanted to get off drugs, but I was having a tough time doing it. I was on the brink of throwing myself over the edge, literally running away from everything—my husband, my mother, everything.

It was such a stressful time for me. In fact, one night between the anxiety from the stress I was experiencing and the pot haze I was in, I ended up in the hospital. I thought I was actually having a heart attack. I learned that the pot was aggravating the stress I was feeling, and that finally gave me the impetus to stop using it.

I knew my mother was walking the edge, and I was walking the edge too. I knew that if I didn't get some real good help for her—well, I didn't know what was going to happen. I felt that the only thing I could do for her at that point was to take her back to church. That was what had brought her around before, and I felt that was the only thing I could do for her.

In taking her back to church, I met my present pastor. He started doing a Bible study with me. Very gradually my faith was rekindled. The month that was the seventh anniversary of the abortion, I started to come to grips with it. I knew we were coming to discussing that in our Bible study, and I knew I was going to have to be forthright about it. When I told him about it, he told me to go to my Lord. He also told me that God can forgive, and he does, but you have to also forgive yourself.

I had asked for forgiveness a few times, but I had never

really accepted forgiveness for myself. I remember at that time that a picture sort of flashed in my mind, a picture of Jesus reaching out to me and saying, "Please take my forgiveness. Don't keep carrying this around with you and stabbing yourself with it. You're only making new wounds."

I realized then that, while I can never take back what I did, I can go forward because God does love me. He did bring me back into his family. If I weren't important, he wouldn't have bothered with me. I thought about him pleading with me to take his forgiveness and the fact that he was willing to take the time to bring me back home. It was a long process—a year and a half to go through all of it—but those were the things that were the healing elements for me.

After I began healing, I tried to bring God's message to my husband. He now has a good relationship with my pastor, and we witness to him all the time. He has also stopped doing the drugs. I would say the spark of faith is there, but he's not willing to acknowledge or admit it yet. There's been a tremendous amount of growth in our relationship, but it's a long process. It takes time and effort and commitment.

I also see the scars from my past life on my children. They have a good relationship with God. They spend a lot of time with the family of faith at church. Still, there's a great deal of anger inside my older son. I worry about that. I think he learned that from me, because that's the way I was through most of his life. Children pick things up from their parents, and that's what he's lived with until recently.

I don't think I'll ever say I'm past the scars. I don't think you can ever say that. You can't take back killing your own baby. After you've had children and developed that bond with them, you realize that's a scar that will always remain. But the way I look at it is, I'm not going to waste any of the gifts God has given me. I'm going to learn from my experiences. Every one of these experiences over the course of my lifetime has had something to teach me. I'm going to take all that, all the struggles and suffering and the growth that has come with it, and use it to the best of my ability to the glory of the Lord. That's where I'm going with my life.

I don't worry about where I am right now as much as I think about where I was and the growth that's been there. I look at that as the positive side of it.

I think many people look at women who have abortions as women who coldly and callously kill their children because they've got something better to do with their lives, but it's not always that way. Many times you have desperate women. That doesn't excuse it, but let's understand that these women don't always want to be where they are.

After my children are a little older I want to get into counseling, working with children from dysfunctional homes, especially young women. It's a sort of prevention.

I really believe that no women escape from the experience of abortion unscathed. Either they deal with the depression and heartache, or they turn themselves into an ice cube and harden themselves so much that they will never let anybody in. I really do believe that. Let's face it: when a woman aborts her child, she kills her child. That sounds really harsh to say, but it's reality. I had to be able to say that, because that's what I had done. Either a woman has to deal with it in those terms or she has to block those emotions out.

The only way I healed was through Christ, and that's what I want to bring into my counseling. I want to point women to Christ, to tell them they already have the tool; they just have to use it.

PENNEY: *I don't think I'll ever say I'm past the scars*

**I will take refuge in the shadow of your wings
until the disaster has passed. (Psalm 57:1)**

my wound ran deep and wide
colored red with pain
tinged by anger
cast in loneliness

inside my ugly adult self
a lonely child lurked silently
waiting to be heard
and comforted and held
hoping someone somewhere
would hear my cry
and understand my pain

but no one heard
or so it seemed
and so I kept on keeping on
no solace for my tears
no freedom from my anger
no shelter from my fears
just a solid shell
around an empty me

and all the while
the wound within
kept festering away
my wound of hurt
and fear
and lonely bitterness

so I fled my fear
and ran from pain
I took my comfort where I could
no price too great to pay
to fill the emptiness within
seeking peace at any cost
I found more hurt instead
more lonely than before

walled up within my guilt
the consequence of death
my baby's death
my wound of shame
the scar I wear
bears silent witness
to my guilt
my never-ending shame

silence child
come soothe your sorrows
ease your pain
find comfort in my love
release from guilt
healing for your wound
of sin and death and shame

I know a thing or two
about that pain
I carried all your sorrows
that day they nailed me up to die
upon my cross

I'm no stranger to the wounds you feel
I bore them all before
your guilt was mine that day
the death you caused was mine to
  bear
stricken, smitten, and afflicted
I was crushed upon that cross
wounded there in shame and death
to free you now from all your guilt
to heal you here within my church
with my forgiving word

I've blotted out your sin
by my own death once long ago
now here receive my life for you
my body broken, blood outpoured
take eat
take drink
and live

that scar is a badge of healing
it testifies of love and joy
my love for you
far deeper than your wound
my joy in you
much higher than your pain

your wound was deep and red
how could there be no scar?
but look again
that scar you wear
now bears the imprint of my cross
a badge of shame no more
it tells of sins erased, forgiven, gone
so take up my cross
and wear it proudly
your scar is now
the emblem of my love

Maria

Maria was reared in a strict, religious home. Her old-world parents had unwavering moral standards, and Maria grew up associating only with people from her own ethnic group and her church, people who shared her parents' moral views.

Leaving behind that rigid world and living on her own, she tried to make up for lost time. "I wanted it all: partying, drinking, having fun," she says. Her rebellion included living with a young man, causing her parents a great deal of shock, grief, and pain.

When she found herself pregnant at 19, with her boyfriend unwilling to assume the responsibility of a child, she faced the choice (as she saw it) of risking her parents' wrath, losing her boyfriend, or having an abortion. She chose the abortion.

Because abortion was still illegal then in her state, she had to play the "game" so her illegal abortion could become legal. That took a long time, however, until it was too late for a simple, early abortion. That's when she entered what she describes as a "scene from hell"—the late abortion ward.

Maria has paid a terrible price for her abortion. Even though it was legal and "clean," a massive infection robbed her of her fertility.

Maria can never undo the effects of that terrible decision, but today, calm in the knowledge she is forgiven and the mother of two adopted children, Maria works with other postabortion mothers.

She and her husband have come to terms with their loss. Yet the pain is always there.

† † † † †

My parents are Serbian, born in Yugoslavia. They escaped to a German refugee camp during World War II and came to the United States in 1950. My oldest brother was born the month after they arrived, and I was born three years later, followed later by two more brothers.

My mother and father were *very* religious people, to the point of being rigid. I can understand why they were that way because I know it was their faith in God that got them through a terrible time in Europe. They lost many family members; the only thing they had to cling to was God.

But, even though I understood, it still wasn't always easy for me. I often felt odd because my parents were foreigners and so different from my schoolmates' parents. Most of my friends were not religious; but I belonged to a "strange" church, and my family was, in the eyes of my friends, overly religious. That made me seem odd to them too.

From the time I was baptized until I was 16 or 17, my whole life revolved around the church. I was in the choir and in a Serbian dance group that traveled around the country. I spent every Sunday at church. My Dad was the cantor, so we had to be there for all the services and often helped him with the music.

I didn't do any regular dating in high school. I was only allowed to do group things, like going to the movies with a bunch of kids from church. As long as the boys were Serbian and my parents knew their parents, it was OK; but dating what my parents called "American boys" was different. Their answer was clear: "Absolutely not."

I wasn't close to my parents emotionally. There were only two emotions allowed in our house—happy and

angry. There was no such thing as sad. That's typical of
concentration camp survivors. They often can't allow
themselves to feel sad. If I felt down about something I
was told, "You have nothing to be sad about. You should
be thankful you have food on the table, clothes on your
back, and a roof over your head."

In our family the sex roles were strictly defined. My
three brothers did boy things, and I was expected to do girl
things. That's the way my parents grew up: women stayed
home and cooked, cleaned, and crocheted while the men
played and worked. There was very little intermingling;
but I was always pretty independent, even rebellious to a
point. I broke minor rules (but never major ones), and
when I disagreed with my parents, I told them why. But, in
the end, I always did what they wanted me to do.

The first time I really crossed the line was when I was
17, and they told me I couldn't date a non-Serbian boy. I
did anyway. There was a lot of tension between my mother and me over that—she was verbally abusive and even
hit me a few times. My father, on the other hand, wasn't
quite so rigid. He told me that he didn't approve of what I
was doing but that he realized I was old enough to do
what I wanted.

The day after I graduated from high school I packed a
bag and left home. I'd worked part-time in the local dime
store since I was 14 and had saved most of my earnings. I
had a job lined up, working for a government-sponsored
project, and it paid good wages. I was able to afford a
small upper flat by myself—in those days rent was cheap.

I had met the father of my child while I was still in high
school. He would occasionally join the group that went
out together, and we were just friends for several years.
Our first official date was after I had graduated and moved
out, around Thanksgiving of 1971. A few months later he
moved into my flat. It wasn't until after he moved in that

we became sexually involved.

It was a scary and confusing time for me. Although I had always had a rebellious attitude, this was my first real act of outright rebellion against my parents, and I knew it. I really loved Sam, but there was a big immaturity factor at work too. It was as if I were saying, "Now that I'm out of the house, I want it all and in five days or less!" I wanted everything, drinking and partying included. Sam had been raised in an alcoholic home, so he knew how to party. We had some good times—or at least I thought they were good.

My parents quickly found out I was living with a man. My mother almost went crazy; she was like a banshee. My father is a little more unconditional with his love. He told me he strongly disapproved of what I was doing, but he said he wanted me closer to home while I was doing it. My parents owned a duplex and lived in the upper flat; the tenant had moved out of the lower flat. Sam and I actually moved into that empty flat. We only stayed about six months before we found our own apartment, but during the whole time my mother never set foot into our flat. She was that hurt and ashamed of what I was doing.

While we were in my parents' flat, I became pregnant. We hadn't been using any form of birth control—we just figured it wouldn't happen to us. At that point Sam and I had known each other for three years and had been living together for six months. I wanted to marry him, but he didn't want to get married.

I was devastated. The sex and the living together meant a commitment to me, but, to him, it didn't seem to. He was very casual about it, like it was just a roof over his head. He said that marriage wasn't even an option, and neither was having a baby.

He came home one night with a card with information on it about legal abortions in New York (this was before

Roe vs. Wade, and abortion was not yet legal). He wanted me to fly to New York alone and have an abortion. I was astounded. I'd never been on an airplane, never even left my home state—and he wanted me to do this alone?

I told him that I didn't think abortion was right and that it wasn't what I wanted. His reply was so logical: we were too young at 19 and 20 to be tied down to kids. Just because I was pregnant was no reason to get married. Two wrongs don't make a right.

I knew in my heart, like so many young, pregnant women, that abortion is wrong. But we all feel trapped—that we have no alternative.

I got daily pressure from Sam. "When are you going to do something?" he'd ask. "You have to do something soon, or it will be too late." I remember at that point being terribly afraid that I would lose him because I wasn't doing what he wanted me to do.

I confided in a friend that I thought I was pregnant and I didn't know what to do. She gave me a card with the name and phone number of a doctor in our own city. I went to him, and he confirmed what I already knew—that I was indeed pregnant, nearly 10 weeks. I started to cry.

My tears provoked an immediate response from the doctor. He said I could have an abortion, and he named a certain number of dollars. I was confused since abortion was still illegal. He told me it could be arranged legally; but I would have to decide in a few days, or it would be too late. He gave me a prescription sheet with several steps written down on it and the amounts of money that would be due at each step.

The first one involved seeing a psychiatrist; he gave me the name and phone number. I went to the psychiatrist the next day. He asked me a list of what seemed like standard questions. If I didn't answer them "correctly," he told me what I should have said and asked the question again.

He told me that, in his opinion, I was too mentally unstable to have children and that I should have a "procedure." He wrote on a piece of paper that I was incompetent to have a baby, and that's how the illegal abortion became legal.

I took the paper back to the original doctor. He said I was too far along to have a suction abortion or a D and C, so he scheduled me at a local hospital for a saline abortion.

I entered the hospital on a hot August day, but I was too frozen inside to even feel the heat. I had to pay a large amount of money, about $600 as I remember, before I could be admitted. Then I was taken to a room where my doctor injected me with saline solution. I was scared to death during the injection, even though it didn't hurt at all. I just lay there, hoping that Sam would come through the door saying, "Stop, this is not the answer." But he didn't.

It was almost like an out-of-body experience. I was on the table, but I was really watching what was happening to me as if I were watching it on TV. I had numbed myself so much that I couldn't feel anything—anything but horror. I was watching what was happening in horror. I remember telling the doctor that this wasn't really what I wanted, but he said that this was the best solution to my problem. "What would your mother and father say if they knew?" he asked.

All through my growing up years I'd been taught to respect doctors, that they would always do what was best for me. I remember thinking that he must be right, that this must be the best solution to my problem. I was mesmerized by these two male authority figures—my boyfriend and my doctor—and I did what they told me to do.

After the injection the doctor sent me home to wait for labor to begin. Cramping started within six hours, while we were at a drive-in movie where Sam had taken me to "cheer me up," and continued for two days. It was the worst two days of my life. I lived on aspirin for the pain. Suicide never entered my mind, but I remember wishing that I would just die and not have to go through with it. I entered the hospital about 2:00 a.m. as the third day was beginning. I was taken to an eight-bed ward which was all women having saline abortions. Many of them were much younger, 13 or 14, and had their mothers with them. I was thankful that my mother wasn't there, that my parents didn't know what I was doing.

That ward was like a scene out of hell. We were left alone, with curtains pulled around our beds for some privacy, until our babies were delivered. Then we were supposed to pull the cord for the nurses to come and clean up. I could hear crying and moaning all around me. I stayed in that bed for over 12 hours and finally, late in the afternoon, delivered the baby. I called the nurse; she put the baby into a steel container and took it away. I saw it, but I didn't see it, strange as that sounds. I knew it was a boy, but I didn't count any fingers or toes, or even relate to the fact that it was my baby. I was in severe denial, and all I kept thinking was, "I have to get through this and just get out of here as fast as I can." Clinging to that thought kept me sane in an insane situation.

After the birth I had a D and C. I remember waking in the recovery room and asking the nurse if I could ever have a baby again. "You'll have to ask your doctor," was all she would say. They wouldn't let me leave the hospital until I could urinate, but I just couldn't, so I had to stay another day.

The next day, when I still had produced no urine, they did some tests and found I had a severe infection—apparently the saline solution had backed up into my tubes. They put me into an ambulance and sent me to another hospital where I was put into intensive care. My kidneys had failed, so they had to put a temporary dialysis tube into my abdomen.

The doctors wanted to call my parents and tell them what had happened. I was so sick I no longer cared about protecting my secret. I was afraid I was going to die, and I wanted my father there. He came right away and just started to weep when he saw me. He had told my mother what was happening, but she didn't want to see me. She was still too angry.

When my kidneys regained function and they removed the dialysis tube, I started bleeding internally and had to have emergency surgery. I came out of surgery with severe jaundice, looking like Kermit the Frog—green. The doctors told my father they didn't think I was going to make it. He called the priest, and I had last rites. That's what finally snapped my mind out of its detached state and put it back into my body—the priest asking if I had anything to confess. Suddenly I realized what I had done to myself, to my baby, to my parents, to the baby's father. It was like dominoes, all the lives that had been affected by what I had done.

I called my mother and told her I wanted to see her. She came to the hospital, and after that she came every day.

I entered the hospital at the end of August; I came home on my birthday, at the end of October. I'd lost over 40 pounds and was so weak I could hardly stand. My parents wanted me to come to their house so they could take care of me, and so I did.

Sam still isn't sure why my father didn't punch him in the nose, but he didn't. He told Sam that we had made a terrible mistake, but it wasn't the end of our lives. He said he and my mother would pray for us and do what they could to help us.

Slowly I got better and regained my strength. In November, Sam and I became engaged and were married in February 1974.

Like many postabortive women I threw myself into my career, keeping myself too busy to think. I worked hard and climbed the ladder at my job. I'd come home, have a couple of drinks to numb the pain, and fall into bed, get up the next morning and repeat the pattern. I was like a robot, but I was functioning and managed to keep myself from going nuts.

My husband, however, slid quickly into alcoholism. I'm sure he felt guilty for having pressured me into the abortion, and I think that set him off. He went kind of crazy with his heavy drinking, got a motorcycle, and had an accident. After that he cut back on his drinking, and things were better; but it wasn't until 1983 that he went into treatment and stopped drinking completely. He's been sober ever since.

In 1978 we started trying to have a family. When a year went by with no pregnancy, we started having tests. The doctors found that, because of the massive infection I'd had, both my tubes were blocked. I had a treatment to open them, but in the process the doctor found severe cysts on one ovary and it had to be removed. The doctor was hopeful I could still conceive with the one ovary, but nothing happened. Tests showed the tube had collapsed again.

Inside, I was devastated by what was happening, by the thought of what I'd done. Now I wanted to become pregnant, and I couldn't. The guilt that I felt, guilt that I'd killed my only child, was extreme. "What kind of a woman am I," I asked myself, "to have allowed such a terrible thing to have happened?"

We had stayed in my parents' church until then, going sporadically, but I knew it wasn't meeting my needs.

Then, that New Year's Eve, my husband and I heard a man, a converted Jew, speak on a religious TV program.

Some of the things he said sparked an interest in me, and I got out my old Sunday school Bible and began reading it. I happened to start with the Gospel of Matthew. Reading that made me realize that Jesus had died for me. He knew about my abortion and had paid for it 2000 years before on the cross. Until that time I had been a nominal Christian. Yes, I believed that Jesus was the Son of God, but it had no personal relevance for me. I remember reading the words, "Your faith has healed you," and searching for any other passage I could find that dealt with healing promises.

At that point God reached out to us, and we found a church that nurtured our faith. I'd like to say that was the end of my struggle with the guilt of my abortion, but it didn't end that quickly.

I knew that I was forgiven by what Christ had done on the cross, but what I couldn't do was forgive myself. I grew up believing that God punishes you for what you do, and, deep inside, I thought this was my punishment for the abortion—not to ever be pregnant again for the rest of my life. I know now that God doesn't do that, that what happened to me was a direct consequence of my choice to have the abortion. I know there are consequences to everything we do in life, and this is one that I am paying.

Even realizing that my infertility was not God's punishment didn't take away the pain. Every month the reminder that I was not pregnant would plunge me into depression. The emotional drain made me tired all the time. I started eating a lot and gained too much weight. I finally went to an infertility specialist and, after tests, she gently told me that I was so filled with scar tissue that she considered pregnancy virtually impossible.

At that point we decided to adopt and went so far as to contract through a lawyer with a pregnant young woman to privately adopt her baby. It cost a lot of money, and the night before we were to get the baby, she changed her mind and decided to keep it. We are still paying on the loan, and every payment is a reminder of another agony.

About that time, I met a woman at a Bible study who had just adopted a beautiful baby from Brazil. I mentioned the idea of overseas adoption to Sam, and he was enthusiastic. It seemed like an answer.

In 1984 we began actively pursuing the overseas adoption. To make a long story short, in 1985 we went to Columbia, South America, and came back with two little girls, sisters, who were about 19 and 29 months old (their ages are estimates, they were abandoned by their mother). They've adjusted wonderfully and are really great kids. They know the whole story of their adoption, and we try to keep it alive for them.

Yet the final resolution of my feelings about the abortion was still to come. One Sunday morning I read in our church bulletin that a local crisis pregnancy line was asking for volunteers. I thought, "Here's a place I could help. I certainly know what a crisis pregnancy is." At the end of their 36-hour training course they told us that, besides pregnant women, they were also beginning to get calls from women who had had abortions. They asked if anyone wanted to volunteer for that work. I knew right away that was where I needed to be.

One of the requirements was that each volunteer go through a healing program based on a Bible study. That's when I finally resolved a lot of things.

All the experts say that healing is a many-step process. You learn that you will always have to live with the consequences of what you've done, but that there are ways to cope with it. For me, that coping process included reconciliation with my aborted baby.

That's hard to do. It's not easy to say, "I took your life— the life of a living human being that was mine." But being able to say it is one step in the healing process.

I've learned a lot over the course of the years since my abortion. The most important thing I've learned is that Jesus Christ is real. He's not just a name, or a statue in front of a church. He was there the day I had my abortion. Even though I didn't have him, he had me.

The second thing I've learned is that abortion is not the answer. It is not a courageous act. Facing your mistake and not taking another life is courageous.

I still can't say, "I'm healed," because healing is a continuing process; but I can say I am healing, and the process will continue until I'm called home.

MARIA: *even though I didn't have him, he had me*

Where can I go from your Spirit?
Where can I flee from your presence? (Psalm 139:7)

where can I go?
I've tried running, Lord
I've made myself busy
with the business of life
but
that's really just busyness
and
it didn't work
all I got was exhaustion

I've tried forgetting
I've made myself look everywhere
except at my distress
but
that's really just hypocrisy
and
it didn't work
all I got was anxiety

I've tried hiding
I've made myself small
so I could cover up my shame
but
that's really just pretending
and
it didn't work
all I got was guilt

so where can I go?
where can I go to hide the shame?
where can I go to forget the distress?
where can I go to run from the
ugliness?

and
where can I go from your Spirit?
where can I flee from your presence?

it's true
I can't get small enough
to hide my sin
I can't think hard enough
to forget my guilt

and thank God
I can't run fast enough
to run away from you

for in my pain
and in my despair
and in my darkness
you are there

your Son invites:
"come to me, everyone weary and
burdened
and I will give you rest"

tired and weary,
I lay down my secret
so ugly, so dark, so vile
it's killing me

"I'll take that sin," he says
"for I have died your death
and I'll make you new and clean
and whole"

and so
I need never hide from sin
I need never shrink from guilt
for if I make my bed in the depths
you are there

what I can never forget
you've already forgiven
the pain that hurts me so
you have borne away
the healing that I long to see
you bring new each day

so where can I go?
nowhere, Lord, except to you
you alone have the words of
    eternal life.

Kelly

Kelly doesn't know how many abortions she's had. She lost count at 10. She knows she had even more, but she's not sure how many.

An abused child, beaten by a mentally ill mother, Kelly looked for self-esteem and closeness wherever she could find it. Often it was in the arms of a man, but, unfortunately, never a man who truly loved and supported her. The men who fathered Kelly's babies used her, traded her intense need for warmth, closeness, and human contact for sex.

Kelly's search for something real and solid to build on led her to seek fame in the world of professional dance, to submit to the multiple abortions, to take cocaine and other drugs, and finally to flee the country in a desperate attempt to find meaning in a life that had burned to ashes around her. "I wasn't even sure I had a soul anymore," she says.

It was in Japan that God found her, in a little mission church among the Buddhist temples. Once he found her, he transformed her life, and she learned that not even 10 or 20 abortions could stand between her and his love.

† † † † †

My family was very fragmented. From the time I was born until I was five years old my mother was in and out of mental institutions. She's been classified as many different things, but basically she's schizophrenic and alcoholic with compulsive behaviors. She would yell at me and beat me to the point where I remember the school nurse asking me where I got the bruises. I didn't really remember where I'd gotten them, because I didn't realize that what my mother did to me wasn't normal. It didn't occur to me, because I didn't know other children were raised differently. Even today it's hard for me to talk about, because she's still very ill. She's always been in such mental anguish.

My father was a typical working-class man. He never got past the seventh grade, but he worked very hard. We lived in a working-class, East-Coast city. He'd leave for work at 5:00 in the morning and come home and just basically want to watch TV and fall asleep on the couch. He and my mother fought a lot.

My grandmother took care of me when my mother just couldn't handle it or was in the hospital. She may have suspected what my mother was doing, but there wasn't anything she could do about it. Family violence just wasn't talked about back then like it is now.

I never considered my life when I was little as being especially unhappy. Yet I never trusted my mother—I still don't—and I remember, as I was growing into my teens, wishing that she would die. I didn't really like her, but I always tried to please her, always felt I *had* to please her. I'd bring her flowers and things. My grandmother would always say, "Your mother can't help it; she's sick." But I never really knew what her problem was until well after I was 20 years old. I never bothered to investigate it before that, because I left home when I was 16.

In high school I always had a boyfriend. I became sexually active at 14, during my freshman year. It was almost against my will; I was pressured into it by my boyfriend. I didn't really get anything out of it. It was just something I did to keep him. I knew about birth control but chose not to use it.

I didn't have much religious background. I went to Sunday school and Bible school with the neighborhood kids when I was very little. I remember earning a Bible. I memorized a verse, Proverbs 23:26, ("My son, give me thine heart and let thine eyes observe my ways") when I was very little, and I never forgot it. But my mother's intellectualizing—she said religion was just a crutch, and I was one of the smart people of the world who didn't need it—had an effect on me. By the time I was a teenager, I despised religion. It was for idiots as far as I was concerned. I was far too smart for that.

I got pregnant the first time at 15. I was terrified because I had read that childbirth was the most painful experience anyone could go through and was terribly dangerous. I was sure it would kill me. I didn't dare tell my mother; I wouldn't get any sympathy from her. I couldn't go to my grandmother either. I felt totally alone and felt I should get myself out of the mess because I had gotten myself into it. I remember that, for my boyfriend, there was no question. I would get an abortion.

It was 1974, right after abortion had been legalized. I called Planned Parenthood. At first they said there was nothing they could do for me because of my age. I pleaded with them, and they referred me to a clinic in another city. The woman told me not to give the real year I was born. They set everything up for me. My boyfriend drove me. I was scared because they said it would hurt a little bit. I didn't want to be knocked out, because I was even more afraid of that. I just kept telling myself that I would be relieved when it was over. I tried to remember what the woman from Planned Parenthood had told me, that the fetus is really just a parasite because it feeds off the mother. I remember that, before she said that, I was on the line, wondering if I was killing something. That statement knocked me over the line, to thinking that it was OK because it wasn't really anything and biologically wasn't even desirable.

I had a suction abortion. It sounds like a vacuum cleaner, and there's a sucking feeling inside your stomach. I was very calm; I'm always in control. They gave me juice and cookies afterwards, and I was greatly, greatly relieved that it was over. But something happened on the way home. We were in a restaurant, and I started crying and laughing hysterically. I kind of lost it for a few minutes. It was kind of weird—a mixture of, in one way, relief and, in another way, mad hysteria. Then we drove home. I went back to school and tried to ignore that it had happened. I continued to date the boy.

I didn't think the abortion had any effect, but that summer I tried to kill myself. I'm not sure I really wanted to die, but I felt different. I had a more pessimistic view of life. One of my friends had said to me, "What's the matter with you, Kelly? It seems like you've lost your bubble."

My mother came to see me in the hospital. I was in a very drugged state, and she started yelling at me, "Why did you do this? You're so stupid!"

A year later I was pregnant by that boyfriend again and had another abortion. Then I stopped dating him and started going with another guy. I had two more abortions of pregnancies by him. They kind of all blur together in your mind after a while.

As I approached high school graduation, I couldn't wait to move out. There was always so much yelling. I just wanted to get away. So I moved in with my third boyfriend. I had one more abortion with him, so by the time I graduated from high school I'd had five. My parents never knew about any of them.

Planned Parenthood was very firm about telling me that I had to use birth control, and they set me up on the pill.

But at that time it wasn't known that antibiotics negate the effect of the pill, and I was taking antibiotics for acne. So I became pregnant even when I was on the pill. I remember telling them that I had taken my pill, every day. I think they thought I was a liar.

That abortion was the worst. I was already five months when I discovered I was pregnant. I was told I had mono, and that's why I wasn't getting my period. I had to be referred to a doctor who was doing second trimester abortions by a method called D and E—dilation and evacuation. They have to dilate the cervix, with a seaweed called laminaria, and then crush the baby's skull so they can get it out. It was far more painful and traumatic, even though the doctor tried to be gentle. I remember that she sat me down and made me promise never to get pregnant again. I just said, "Yeah, yeah."

I didn't have a very good self-image at that time. I was training to be a professional dancer, and that's all I cared about. I always saw myself as a loner. A few friends knew about the abortions. I didn't want it to get to other people because I was afraid of getting flack about it, but it really was no big deal for me. I don't remember feeling any guilt; I just felt stupid for letting myself get caught so many times. Any guilt I may have felt I totally buried underneath, or it would have driven me crazy. I just ignored the question of whether or not it was a life I was killing. I guess I knew that, if I ever addressed that question, I wouldn't be able to bear it. It was always easier to get an abortion than to find a loving person to be in a relationship with.

I didn't go on to college after high school. My parents said they didn't have the money, so I should forget it, and I'd never been taught to work toward a goal. I also hated school; I hated it so much. So I got a job and continued working toward my dance career. I wanted to save money so I could move to New York.

I had another boyfriend the last few years I lived in my hometown. I lived with him. I had a couple more abortions. They get really blurry here.

I had several other boyfriends after him and several more abortions. I'd given up on birth control at that point; I figured it didn't work anyway. Sex was incredibly important to me—to be close to somebody. As a dancer I was a very physical person, and in its purest sense it wasn't sex at all. I just wanted to hang on to somebody, to have physical closeness. I also wanted the attention.

I honestly don't remember how many abortions I had, but I know I was getting sick of it. I remember counting up once and it was at least ten. I know I thought that, if you'd lost count in your own head, it had to be too many.

I never mourned or grieved for an abortion. I'd become upset sometimes. I remember thinking what a rotten life it was; but I didn't see that I was in a destructive pattern, so I never went for any counseling to see how to stop it.

Then I moved to New York. The first year I didn't go out with anybody. I was very lonely. I worked as an usher at Radio City Music Hall and continued with dance classes, but it wasn't going very well. I was sick; I wasn't eating right. I started working for an administrator at the music hall. Everyone thought that was really great, but I didn't feel good about it because I felt I should really be on the stage side.

I met a man then, a stagehand at the theater, and very soon afterward became pregnant. That started it all over again. I'm not even sure what year it was, but I was in my early 20's. I remember I told him that I get pregnant very easily, and I asked him what he would do if I did. He said he'd marry me, of course. But when it happened he wanted me to get an abortion. I was in love with that man, and I remember, before I had the abortion, I prayed to God

133

and asked him to forgive me for what I was going to do and asked him to take care of that child. I grieved after that one. I remember thinking, "That poor little baby never had a chance."

There were other factors too, that I don't want to go into here—many drugs, a serious cocaine addiction—that were part of my life in New York.

There were also other men. I know I had one more abortion during that time, from a man I'd only been with once. I remember thinking, "Well, you played; now you've got to pay."

In some ways it was as if I was living a double life, because I was keeping all this from my parents and other relatives. I remember thinking that it wasn't right; but, at the same time, if I could just hold it together, it would suit me fine.

I was getting tired of New York by then, tired of the city and tired of not getting enough work as a professional dancer, of living on unemployment. I was still hung up on that one guy, the one I loved. I knew he loved me too, but he just couldn't seem to ask me to marry him. So I started thinking about leaving the country, broadening my horizons and seeing the world.

I decided to go to Japan, because it was the farthest place away that I could think of. I did my homework; I didn't leave with no plans. I left New York and lived with my grandmother for six months, saving money. When I had enough, I got on the plane. I had the name of a place to stay and a book about getting a job in Japan. They're starved over there for people to teach English. When I arrived, I was treated with the highest regard. I started teaching English, but I ended up starting a dance company and doing work in television, mostly commercials.

I know I was searching for something. At that point I wasn't sure I even had a soul. I thought, "I have to find my soul on this trip before I can go back to America." Eastern religions had always interested me, so I listened to the Buddhist's chant and tried to understand what keeps the Japanese going; but it didn't fulfill me. I remember being so disappointed and thinking, "Here I've traveled all these miles, and their philosophy is just as stupid as any I've ever known."

Then a Canadian friend I'd met there became a Christian through a mission project from the United States. I wondered, "How can this intelligent lady become a Christian?" In my circle, especially the theater and dance world, Christianity is like a poison. You just don't associate with those people—maybe there's something about them that makes you condemn yourself, so you don't want to be around them—I don't know. I remember feeling sad that she had become a Christian and hoping that she wouldn't start in on me. But she did tell me about it, and I figured I'd have to go to church with her sometime so I wouldn't offend her. She wasn't a high pressure person; she always presented everything very quietly and nicely.

I was trying not to think about it, but my guilt was starting to come up. I felt that I was being crushed by a tremendous weight of guilt. I couldn't seem to escape it. I remember one night walking alone down by the river, crying and trying to count all the abortions I had. I knew I needed forgiveness, but I didn't know how to get it.

Then one night my friend and I were sitting around her house, and she was reading the Bible. For some reason, all the guilt for my abortions, all my feelings about my past, starting coming to my mind again. She was reading the part where Jesus says that, if any man thirst, he should come and Jesus would give him a drink of living water. I remember that I finally understood what he was talking about. I understood what he was saying; I understood it spiritually. It wasn't just reading a book.

Something happened that night. I went home to my little cubby-hole house. I knew that my grandmother had sent me a Bible at one point. When I had gotten it I thought, "I wish this sweet old lady hadn't wasted her money sending me this stuff." When I got home I tore the house apart until three in the morning, trying to find that Bible. Do you think I could find it? I was in tears. I called my friend the next morning, and she got me a Bible. I started reading it.

I started going to the church, which met in an American club, with my friend. At first I was thinking, "Oh, these people are just whacked out," because everyone was so happy to be there. The love of God just shone through them and the minister. At the same time I was quite attracted, wanting to know what they had. What they had, I found out, was Christ. I'm not sure I fully understood God's plan of salvation then, but it was enough to realize that Jesus is Lord and he cared about me and forgave me for my sins.

After that, Christ was with me. I realized that I never would be alone again and that all the horrible sins I had committed, including the abortions, were forgiven. I knew Jesus loved me, and that was the love I'd been looking for all those years. It all became clear to me in the matter of just a few months. I became so happy. I called my grandmother, and she was happy for me. I wrote all my friends in New York; they were confused by it.

I felt, then, that my life as a dancer was over. I no longer enjoyed it, and I was approaching the end of my twenties, which is the end of a dancer's prime. I realized it was time to move on to a new career.

So I came home from Japan. I realized I had a whole life ahead of me, and I wanted to share it with someone who felt the same way about God. I trusted that God would put me in the right place sooner or later. I lived in New York, working as a park ranger for the summer and taking courses in landscape design.

I had one more thing to deal with—the man I had been pining away for, for so many years. He'd heard that I was back and called me. I remember knowing in my heart that it wasn't going to work, but hoping that he would listen to my story, and I could share my faith with him. It didn't work. I was devastated once more.

I prayed to God, saying, "Wouldn't it be nice if I could meet a man who is interested in the same things I am, who is a Christian?" At the same time, I did think that perhaps I was one of those women who would never marry. I remember thinking that if that's what God wanted for me, that was OK too. But within three months of that prayer, I went on a vacation to Arizona and flopped with a friend of mine who lives there. She introduced me to a Christian man, who was an architect.

I'm married to him now, and we have a son. We just clicked. It happened so fast, we were married after we saw each other just six times, as I flew back and forth between New York and Arizona. It seemed like we felt married after our first two times together.

Our son is our pride and joy. I look at him and can't believe I did the things I did. But, in my own heart, I'm certain of forgiveness. I still regret it; there's still pain. If I allowed myself to dwell on it, it could be bad again, but I don't think God wants that. It's over. God gives complete forgiveness and complete rest. He's the only one that could heal me. He's the only one who can heal anyone.

I'm not sure what would have happened to me if it weren't for God. I remember thinking in my early 20's that I wasn't going to live past 29 anyway, so it didn't matter. Still, I had come pretty far through sheer willpower, even before God came into my life. I'd gotten over my drug problems and wised up to the effects of abuse by reading a lot about having an abusive and alcoholic parent. So I might still be alive, but I know I would be leading a pretty miserable life.

Today I'm 31 and I'm very happy. I run a day-care center in my home, and we're thinking about adopting some more children.

From the experiences in my life I've learned that God always gives you choices, and he always gives you the right choice. Often it's the more difficult choice, but it's the one that makes you stronger afterwards. My self-esteem is slowly getting better. I've become more hard-headed; I don't want to be a wishy-washy Christian. I want to stand up for what I believe. My experiences have given me the courage to live my life out loud rather than in a closet.

KELLY: *I knew I needed forgiveness, but I didn't know how to get it*

If you, O LORD, kept a record of sins, O LORD, who could stand?
But with you there is forgiveness;
therefore you are feared. (Psalm 130:3-4)

memory is kind
it masks out pain
but can't erase it
looking back I see a haze
sometimes when I'm strong
I peer inside that haze
and see there dimly outlined shadows
fuzzy portraits from my past
faded snapshots of my life
yellowed, wrinkled, dim with years
but the pain is bright and sharp
in hues of red
the color of my sin

images float by as on a screen
childhood fears
adolescent struggle
a mother's ranting
a father's silence

a child sits all alone
watching, weeping, wondering why
longing for tranquility
yearning for relief and shelter
finding none

a teen sits in the darkness
this snapshot dark and sinister
the loneliness in sharper outline
the soul more undefined
inside that tortured adolescent mind
a scheme takes shape
first hurt, then hate,
then vengeance plotted
but never executed

turning pages from my album
scenes fade faster still
a hectic pace
a frantic life
a frenzied blur
but from each frozen portrait of
  adulthood
a face peers out at me
that same lonely, frightened face
that child in tears
that teen wrapped up
in pain and hate
they're all the same
from each snapshot in my book
the same face stares at me
my ugly face
my frightened, angry, ugly face

I longed to please
I yearned for closeness
I searched for love
but settled for much less
the touch of flesh
my surrogate reality
afraid to face my past
I ran from life
ran fast and hard and far

I used men's bodies
to escape the pain
and they used mine
there were babies too
their bodies used and trashed
emptied and discarded
the throwaways of ugliness
my ugliness and sin

the pictures fade and dim with age
faceless men haunt my dreams
nameless children deprived of life
one immense collage of ugliness
with guilt inscribed on every page
the private album of my sin

now come, my child
give me that book
let's turn its pages one by one
and look unflinchingly at sin
nothing's hid from me, you know

I know you now
I knew you then
you've nothing more to hide from me
I've seen them all before
each ugly photograph
every snapshot from your painful life
each record of your sin
no need of holding back from me

for I've a Word for you
he's my own Word in human flesh
all my fullness lives in him
and he is life for you
for all the ugly guilt of all the world
was laid on him
including all the scenes
you hide in shame
those portraits of your sin
are hid in him

my Word of life in skin and bones
is life for you in spoken word
in water, bread, and wine
the channels here and now
of my deep love embodied there
    and then
in his cross of death
and open tomb of life

his risen life is life for you
for you have drowned and died
    with him
his pure and holy bride
he feeds you in his wedding feast
with body broken, blood outpoured
his signet seal of love

look again, my love
at the album of your life
you're afraid it's stained with guilt
but open it and look with me
come, see on every page
the Bridegroom's blood
blots out your sin
you're clean and pure
in him

Marilyn

Marilyn is beautiful. Now in her mid-twenties, she has perfect, creamy skin; enormous, slightly almond-shaped green eyes; and short dark hair that sweeps back in layered wings, accenting her high cheekbones. Photos of her from her younger years show two different Marilyns. In one she's a teenage girl with long, flowing dark hair, holding a flower next to her face. She's as lovely and fragile as the blossom. The other shows Marilyn ready to go out with one of her gay male friends. Her punk make-up— white face, bright red lips, and spiked black hair—look tough and defiant.

That's the dichotomy of Marilyn: beautiful, but never sure she could attract a man who would truly love her; quick-witted, but with a hard, sharp edge; someone who thought sex was the antidote for alienation.

Today Marilyn is married. She and her graduate-student husband have two children. Reflecting her love for music, opera floats through their small apartment. She speaks softly. Her perfect diction and effortless flow of words testify to her intelligence. Often, however, the flow of words is choked by tears. At some points she pauses, overcome, unable to go on. Her tears are for the baby she aborted while she was pulled between her two selves: the baby, she says, whose beating heart she stopped, the baby who still haunts her mind every time she reads a pro-life ad.

† † † † †

I grew up in the desert of the Southwest, the last child of five. My oldest sister is 20 years older than I am. My father was in both World War II and Korea. He was shell-shocked; his helmet was shot off five times. I think you could describe him as eccentric, difficult.

He retired from the service just before I turned a year old. My parents went through a lot of hard times because after the war he couldn't find a job, and by then they had five children to support. I remember when I was about four, when my father came home, I hid from him because I didn't like kissing him. I was almost afraid of him. The only time I remember him telling me he loved me was once during my teenage years. On my wedding day he took me aside and said, "I want you to have this," and he gave me $50. It really hit home then that he did love me. But I was not close to him, not as far as sharing my life with him. He just gets everything so convoluted and doesn't understand how real life is.

My mother—my long-suffering mother—was 42 when I was born. She says that I kept her young. I was always close to her. I think my brothers and sisters feel I'm her favorite and that she indulges me. They are right in some ways, but Mom and I had some rough times there for a while when I was in my teens.

I was raised in a strict, fundamentalist church. I remember at about age three or four realizing that I loved Jesus and that he loved me. I did a lot of Bible study as I was growing up. I felt very committed to being a Christian; but when I was about 13, our church got a new pastor, and he split the church. I became very bitter, not toward God but toward the organized church, and I stopped going.

When I was in high school, guys were afraid of me, I think. I always looked older than I was, and I was really smart. They would try to play one-up with me, and I would always win! I think I was intimidating.

When I was 16, I met a guy named Kyle, and we dated quite a bit. He was a classical pianist, and I was a singer. I was really in love with him, as you can only be at 16, but there was something strange about our relationship. There wasn't much physical feeling; it was mostly emotional. During the two years I dated Kyle, I asked him again and again if he was gay. He out-and-out lied to me, because he really was. So, at a critical time in my life, I was dating someone who wasn't giving me a sense of self-worth as a woman. He wasn't interested in me physically; and I think some of the things I did during that time, and after we broke up, I did because I didn't feel sexy or desirable as a woman.

During my junior and senior years in high school, while I was dating Kyle, I really fell away from the church. I dabbled a little in mysticism and "white" witchcraft, although I continued to consider myself a Christian.

I did a lot of drinking too, starting at age 15. I looked as old then as I do now. I could get into bars with no problems. But I never took drugs. I was always afraid of them because I felt I had too much potential to blow myself away.

The week after I graduated from high school, I set out to lose my virginity. My mother had never talked to me about sex, never said anything about how you get pregnant or how you prevent it. I didn't feel like I was attractive to men, even though I was always getting whistled at. I never believed that a man could be attracted to me because the one I felt closest to was not. I met a man in a bar. He was in his early 40s, and we had a sexual relationship off and on that summer.

Then I started college at the state university, though I continued living at home. There I quickly became what the kids called a "fag hag"—the token woman in a group of male homosexuals. They were my friends, and it was a safe place for me to be. I was still sort of dating Kyle at that time, although I was also having one-night-stands with other men all over the place.

One night I was in a gay bar with my friends, and a man came up to me and said, "I think you should know that I saw Kyle on a date with another guy." I knew it inside, I guess, but I didn't want to know it. That's when I broke up with him.

In the spring of my freshman year, I spent a lot of time in the student union. My gay friends had a table there, and we would hang out between classes. I met this Greek guy and dated him a few times. We only had sex twice; then he dropped me like a hot potato. I think he had someone back in Greece. I didn't really care because there wasn't any emotional tie between us. Sex for me at that time was just a way to be close to somebody. I was very lonely, even though I had many friends.

I had been on the birth control pill earlier, but my mother put up such a big stink about it that I finally had to go off it. So I wasn't using anything. In late March, I found out I was pregnant. I just cried. I went to one of my gay friends, and he said, "Whatever you want to do, I'll help you." He comforted me, hugged me, offered to pay for an abortion if I wanted one.

I didn't know what to do. With my mother's attitude about birth control pills, I certainly couldn't tell her I was pregnant. It would have been so awful; I was sure they'd kick me out of the house. I couldn't picture them, at age 60, raising a child. I couldn't picture myself raising a child either. You know, you think you're so mature at that age. You do all these "mature" things—drinking and going to bars; but when the time comes to find out if you really are mature, you discover you're not.

I thought briefly of having the baby and giving it up for adoption, but I couldn't imagine myself staying home pregnant until I had it. I didn't realize there were places you could go. I knew the baby would be beautiful—the father was very good looking with green eyes and dark, curly hair. I thought, if I had it, I wouldn't want to give it up. No matter which way you go in this situation, you are going to pay for it.

I knew that, if I was going to have an abortion, I had to do it right away before it "became a baby." I thought, if I could get rid of it before it was really a baby, it would be OK.

So I called my gay friend again. I'd found out that I could get an abortion for $110 at Planned Parenthood. I asked him if he'd go with me and told him how much money I'd need. He said he'd give it to me. I made the appointment for the first week in April. He drove me there and waited for me.

There were about six women in the group. We all had to tell why we were going to have the abortion. I think they wanted to make sure that no one was forcing us into it. One woman was married to a man who worked in a cemetery. I remember thinking how ironic that was. I was just incredulous that she would have an abortion when she was married, just because it wasn't the right time to have a baby. That was hard to understand when, for myself, I felt I had no other way out. I had no husband, no means of support. That was all the counseling except for explaining the procedure. We sat there silently while they called us one by one. What was there to say?

I was one of the last ones called. I got undressed, put on a hospital gown, and got up on the table. There was a nurse holding my hand and talking to me to distract me from what the doctor was doing. I remember that it hurt. I remember that . . . sucking . . . sound. I can still . . . hear it. I will hear it for the rest of my life. When the instrument tears . . . (I'm sorry) . . . apart the fetal tissue, I can't even describe that sound. It felt like the doctor was scraping around in my uterus to get every last bit.

But finally it was over with.

They took me out into a waiting room. There were juice and cookies and stuff, and I had to lie there for a while. Then they let me go. My friend took me to MacDonald's and fed me. Then I went back to school.

The immediate feeling was one of relief. It had solved a big problem for me, or so I thought at the time. I was very relieved and almost happy, so everything I was feeling I just kept inside. I think my gay friends all found out, and they were very nice to me; but we never *talked* about it.

There was a dichotomy going in me at that point. A part of me, a very small part to be sure, was still a child of God and knew that what I had done was wrong. But most of me had fallen away, and I had a very good rationale—I had many good reasons to have an abortion at that point in my life. I'm sure my reasons weren't any different than those of anyone else who is having an abortion today. I just finished the school year and went on my merry way. It didn't seem to affect me very much.

I did finally tell the father I had gotten pregnant. I saw him with his gang in the "Greek quarter" of the union. I asked if I could talk to him alone. "The last time we had sex I got pregnant, and I had an abortion a week ago," I told him. What could he say? He said, "Thank you." I thought it was an odd response. I hadn't told him earlier because I knew he was in the middle of midterms and was under a lot of pressure. I really don't know why I was so concerned about him, when it should have been the reverse; but I never gave him that chance. I think he was probably relieved that I had taken care of it, and he didn't have to worry about it.

One direct effect it had on me was that I drank more. I never did drink to being falling-down drunk. I just drank to the point that I would feel good and forget—not specifically the abortion—but forget the way my life was at that point. I was really scraping the bottom of the barrel.

I started going out with a guy named Jay. He was gay, but I knew it. He didn't want gay relationships because he was afraid of AIDS. He just wanted somebody to go out with him for fun. He'd do my hair, and we'd make the rounds of the bars. We were really close friends, and we weren't playing any sexual games. I'd still have an occasional one-night-stand; but they were a lot fewer, and I was taking precautions not to become pregnant again.

That summer I was taking voice lessons at the university. There was a man, an organ major, who had the lesson after mine. He kept coming earlier and earlier to listen to me sing. When school started in the fall, I ran into him almost everywhere I went. It was the weirdest thing. I thought, "There's got to be reason why I keep running into this guy." But I couldn't remember his name! Once when I ran into him, I gave him my phone number and hoped he'd call.

I wasn't happy where I was at that time. I felt stuck in a lifestyle I'd created and the persona that I'd created for myself. With my punk look, I was a caricature of the person I really was, but all my friends knew me as that person. They didn't know Marilyn. I knew changing would be very difficult, but I knew that inside I wanted to change. I wanted to get out of the bar scene. I'd never had a long-term relationship even though I had many male friends and had had a lot of sex. But all the men who had sex with me liked the way I looked—the pretty face—and the way I dressed. They were attracted to me, we had sex, and that was it. It was a pattern.

When I met Paul, it was different. He did call, and we had a few dates. One day at lunch I told him, "I'd really like to go to bed with you." He said no. I was shocked, absolutely shocked! He told me that I was a very attractive woman and he was attracted to me, but he wasn't going to have sex until he was married.

The more I thought about that, the better it sounded, because no man had ever taken the time to find out about Marilyn before he took Marilyn to bed. None of them had taken time to look beyond the pretty face and the sparkly wit, and really talk to me. He did.

We became very, very good friends. Our first date was in September. By the end of November we were seeing each other every day. We got engaged on Christmas Eve and married the next May.

While we were dating, I decided that it was important for him to know me as well as he possibly could. I didn't want to have any secrets or surprises after we were married. I felt that if it wasn't going to work out because of the things I had done, I wanted it to end before I was really hurt. At lunch one day in November, I said, "I have something to tell you, and it's not going to be easy for me to say." I started by telling him that I had been with many men, which I think he had already guessed. Then I told him that I'd had an . . . abortion. He was . . . shocked. Then he asked me if I knew God.

"Of course. I'm a Christian," I said.

"You are?" he asked.

Then I realized, full force, what my life was like and how far from God I really was. I really began to feel the . . . separation between me and God.

Paul knew me as a loving, sensitive person and said he didn't understand how I could have done that. I could only answer, "I don't know either. How could I?" At that point it started to come home to me, just what I had . . . done eight months earlier.

One night shortly after that, I had a dream. In my dream there were two paths: On one path I saw Paul and marriage and children. On the other path I saw my gay friends, my drinking . . . and death. I think if I had chosen to continue my life as it was, I would have been dead. I don't think I could have kept going as I was.

A few weeks later, I had another dream. Before going to bed, I had been praying about all the sins I had committed. In my dream I saw an island. Around it was a huge chasm, bottomless. I knew God was on the island. There was peace and love there, but there was no way across the chasm. But then Christ was there, standing in front of me with his arms outstretched, and he made a bridge across that chasm for me to get to God. I began to walk across, and that was the end of the dream.

From that point on, things were different. I began to go to church with Paul. I heard the law and I heard the gospel, and it seemed as if every Sunday the message was just for me.

Paul and I both really believe that God brought us together, and we have fulfilled needs in each other. We have two little girls now, age four and a baby.

I know now that my abortion is forgiven. I know intellectually that there is no difference in sins to God. But what makes it so hard is that it's such a personal sin, and it's so hard to forgive myself.

It was hard when I was pregnant with my first daughter. I remember wondering what that first baby would have looked like. One of the questions they ask is how many pregnancies you've had. I didn't feel I could lie, so it was on my chart. While I was in labor a resident came in and said, "I see you've had an abortion. Is there any medical problem I should know about?" I wanted to strangle him.

For some reason it was even harder to deal with during my second pregnancy. The first one was so easy, no medical problems at all; but I had several physical problems during the second pregnancy. I was in a serious car accident that cracked a rib. I developed asthma and had some other problems. Again that question, "How many pregnancies have you had?" I had a lot more feelings, unresolved things. I thought it was strange—after all, by then the abortion had been six years earlier—but every time I saw an ad against abortion (and that still happens), there was something that shot through me. I remember once driving down the highway and seeing a billboard that said "Abortion Stops a Beating Heart" and thinking, "I did that." I will forever . . . regret it.

I think the whole experience has made me realize just how human I really am and how much I need Christ.

There are so many things in your life having an abortion can affect. How do you tell someone you love deeply that you've done something like that? Or do you tell him at all? Abortion can affect your ability to have another child, your deepest emotions, and, certainly, your marriage.

I think any woman who is raised with even the most basic moral values, even if she's not a Christian, will have some trouble after having an abortion.

Abortion doesn't solve problems, although it may seem to at first. It only compounds them, and it isn't worth the lifelong pain. I'm one of the lucky ones. I came out of this with a good marriage and two healthy, beautiful children. But it's always there. The abortion will always be in the back of my mind. I'm not sure I'll ever have total peace until I go to heaven.

MARILYN: *I don't think I could have kept going as I was*

Out of the depths I cry to you, O Lord. (Psalm 130:1)

it was all a game
a game called let's pretend
or
can you tell me who I am

I looked into my mirror
and saw
a girl I didn't know
and so
I kept on looking
searching the eyes of others
for some dim reflection
to catch a glimpse of me

I tried so hard to please
it was just another game
called masquerade
complete with costume
hair and makeup
carefully selected
for just the right effect
a cleverly devised disguise
to cover up the person
who lived inside of me

I tried on strange relationships
hoping for security
clinging to the fringe groups
someplace safe, I thought
if I were weird enough
no one would bother me
a complicated masquerade
a careful dance
with exhausting choreography

but I danced on
looking for my true identity
can you tell me who I am

I asked all those men
they looked, I gave, they took
but no one looked beyond my body
no one knew my heart
and I danced on alone
I played the part
but not so well

a demanding drama
a consuming role
I played the part
I acted out my role
so carefully
but to an empty hall
and after all was over
no applause
only silence
my costumed self
an empty caricature
a vacant shell

silence, child
I know you well
I made you first
and formed you
within your mother's womb

stop the masquerade
quit your tiring game
halt the complicated dance
ring down the curtain on your act

no more pretending now
take off your mask
undo the costume
step out of it

and into life
my life, and live for real
free and alive in me

don't hide your eyes
from cruel reality
now take a look
a careful look
at all your sin
then look again
at me
open wide your eyes
and see my cross
where I covered all your sin
in my own blood
in water and in word
buried with me in my own death
and out again to life
my hidden life

so now you're safe
you're hid in me
no acting now
at last you're real
you're free

Sarah

Many people would feel that Sarah had a good reason to have an abortion. The child she was carrying had only a 25 percent chance of being born normal because of radiation treatments her husband had received. Doctors told her to terminate her pregnancy. Friends and relatives told her it was the only thing to do. Even her ministers told her to do what the doctor thought best.

What other people think about the rightness or wrongness of Sarah's decision doesn't matter, however. Sarah did what her conscience told her not to do, and the resulting pain and grief are very real to her.

Sarah, now age 56, has always regretted ending the pregnancy, even though she knows the child could have been born severely handicapped. She carried her pain inside until the June when the child would have graduated from high school. Then, in a time of parties and beginnings, Sarah faced an ending.

† † † † †

My kids say that I broke the mold in my family. My sister is unhappy in her marriage. My parents have been unhappily married for 62 years. It was like I said, "I'm going to be happy in spite of you." I made my own happiness, with the help of God, of course.

There was a lot of tension in my home because of my parents not getting along—most of the time they weren't speaking to each other. I got away from it through my dog

153

and cat, my garden, and the big swing on the end of our barn. The swing was so high I could see the skyline of Detroit. I entertained myself and just stayed away from my parents.

I could never talk to them about sex. Never. One day when I saw two cats mating, I pointed it out to my sister, and she said, "Don't look at that!" My mother right away rushed me away. That was the first information I ever had; I must have been about nine at the time.

I was really happy in high school. I had lots of friends. I was on the year book staff and the debate team, and I enjoyed it all very much. I met my husband, Frank, at the library window during my sophomore year. We became very good friends and got married three years later, ten days after I graduated. That's what you did in our town back in the 50's. Hardly anybody went on to school. You just got married.

We were sexually active before we got married, but he was the only one. It was troubling for me. We were a religious family, always went to church. Every week I would resolve not to do that again, and the next week we'd fall into it again. It was very difficult. My husband didn't have conscience pangs then, but looking back now, he says, "We were so stupid!"

We were married nine months and 13 days before our first baby came along. I had a miscarriage after that and then two more children, with a total of eight years between them. We were very happy, oh yes, truly happy. We've been married 39 years now.

But when Frank was 34, he had cancer in the reproductive organs. They had to take a testicle and give him radiation treatments. They told us, if we wanted any more children, we'd better do it before the treatments started, because once he'd had the radiation he would be sterile. At that time our oldest daughter was 14; the middle one,

10; and the youngest, six. I had quite difficult pregnancies, and we have a blood incompatibility similar to the Rh factor. Each child had more of a chance of having blood problems, so we didn't plan on having any more.

My husband had the surgery and radiation treatment. Afterwards he had a sperm count done and was absolute zero. That was in 1968. Four years later, in 1972, we had an especially difficult year. Frank lost his job, and it was a very rough time for him. A year into his job loss, I became pregnant. I thought I had the flu, but when I went to the doctor, he told me I was pregnant. "That's not possible," I said, "my husband is sterile." But he replied, "Honey, no matter whose it is, you're pregnant."

I didn't know how to tell my husband, but I finally did. He went for another sperm count. Normal is over a million—he had a count of six. If we had been applying for adoption, he would have been considered sterile! But somehow I got pregnant with that low sperm count. At first we were just dumbfounded, but later we were happy, thinking, "Well, this was unplanned, but won't it be nice? It will be fun."

But the doctors sobered us up real quick by telling us that the baby stood little or no chance of being normal because of the radiation. Radiation damages the sack where the sperm are formed so even new sperm are not normal. That really hit us something fierce. We were absolutely devastated. We went for genetic counseling at the University of Michigan, and 14 doctors confirmed the danger and said we should not have the baby. They said the burden on the family was so great that it would not be a wise thing to do.

At that time abortion was not legal in Michigan. It was only legal in New York. The doctors gave me the names of some people in New York to see.

With that I left the clinic and went to see my minister.

155

First I saw an older minister, a man in his seventies. He told me that he thought I should listen to the doctors, but that wasn't what I wanted to hear. I really wanted this baby, and I wanted someone on my side.

So I went to a younger minister, but he said the same thing, that I should listen to the doctors. I left, thinking that no one was really saying what I wanted them to say.

My husband was afraid. I was so sick; I'd lost so much weight. He didn't have a job. He said, "I can't bear the thought of me not having a job and then losing you, too." He never gave me an ultimatum, but he was so grieved. The loss of his job had devastated him, and our insurance and everything was done within 24 hours. He also wasn't sure he was really over the cancer.

So I talked to the people in New York. A woman there told me that I wasn't pregnant yet, but there was some tissue there, and if I didn't do something soon, I would be pregnant. I remember thinking to myself, "I'm 37 years old. How stupid do you think I am?"

I went through such terrible stress and conflict between the pressures of the doctors, the ministers, my husband, and other relatives and friends who knew about it. I was baby-sitting at the time for a lady who lived down the street who had a child with a genetic bone disease that caused deformities. Jenny was the dearest little thing, with quite a tremendous IQ. The woman said to me, "Sarah, I'm begging you. Do you think Jenny's happy? Do you think I'm happy? Do you think my husband is happy? Don't go through with this and have a deformed child."

So, because of all the pressures, I went against my conscience and went to New York and had the abortion. To this day I regret it, and I will until the day I die.

The procedure was horrid. I was 37 years old, and there I was with all these teenagers. One girl was there with her father, who made her walk through the door while she was shouting, "I don't want to do this, I don't want to!" It was a horrible scene.

We had to all line up, take our clothes off, and put them in shopping bags with string handles and put on hospital gowns. They called us in when they were ready. The nurse held on to my hand while the doctor dilated me with no anesthetic whatsoever. They didn't want anybody lying around who was groggy. Afterwards they did counseling about birth control. They took cash only, and we were in and out of there in less than two hours.

I had such an empty feeling when it was over. I had no pain, no bleeding, just a void like I've never felt in my life.

I didn't sleep that night. I'll never forget it. I was high in a hotel above Central Park and could hear screaming and crying from somewhere across the hotel. I heard it all night long. My conscience was so troubled.

I had asked the doctors, when they were advising me to get the abortion, why I couldn't wait until the baby was born and, if it was terribly deformed, let God take it then. They looked at me as if to say, "Are you crazy, lady?" They couldn't understand my reasoning. But I kept thinking, "What's the difference if you kill a baby after it's born or if you kill it before?" I felt that way then, and I still do.

When I got back, my husband was very quiet. I can't say to this day if he was sad, relieved, or what; but I couldn't turn to him for comfort. He was just ignoring that it ever happened. The two older children knew what had happened. The middle one, who was 14 then, had said to me before the abortion, "Mom, if it's born with no hair or something, we'll buy something to fix it." He was just so tenderhearted. I felt so bad that he knew about it. He knew too much.

Later I apologized to the children for what I had done, and they all said they understood and forgave me.

For about the first fifteen years after the abortion, I let

people comfort me by saying that what I did was not wrong. I'd say, "Well, my abortion was a little different." But it really was no different. No, this was a human being, and I played God.

I realized we truly did have a problem, a very weighty one; but that didn't comfort me. I'd rather have had the baby born, and if it truly was in such distress, God would have taken it. Or, with our help, it would have survived.

Every May third it rocked me, plus many times in between. I never forgot it. During those years, I continued to go to church. The ministers knew about it. In fact, the younger one baby-sat for our children while I was gone. They asked if I wanted to talk again, and I said that I thought they had covered the subject the first time. Nothing was ever mentioned again, it was like it didn't happen.

I had to buck up and be the strong one. I never broke down for 18 years.

Then, this past June, when all the graduations were in the paper and everyone was having parties, I thought, "This would have been the year." I don't know why. It wasn't Christmas. It wasn't when that baby would have been born. It was when it would have graduated. I cried every day for months, and I'm not a person who usually does that. I've always been strong. I didn't even let my husband know how it was bothering me, even though we are so close.

I needed someone to talk to and got comfort long-distance from my son and his minister. The minister counseled me over the telephone and through letters, and he brought me out of it. He told me I was what he called an "overly proud sinner." He said, "You can't believe that you, Sarah, would ever do something like that in your whole life. But you are no different than any other person; we are all sinners."

That brought me back into the world. He was right. I was thinking, "But you are such a good Christian, how could you ever have let this happen?" I knew I was forgiven, that God had forgiven me years ago; but I couldn't accept that forgiveness for myself. That changed when he told me that pride was at the root of it, and it was like a light bulb that came on. When I saw that I was no different from any other person, then I could accept that I had slipped and done something so horrid. Then I could forgive myself.

Since then I've had a chance to meet that minister and shake his hand and thank him.

Now my conscience is clear, but the grief will never leave. I will always grieve for the face that's not at the table.

Today I fill my hours with happy thoughts. I have a close relationship with my seven grandchildren. I still think about the abortion, maybe once a week or so, but I don't sit and cry about it any more. I would say I'm healed.

Many people think that I did exactly what I should have done, but I have to tell people that it maybe wasn't the right thing, in fact, *for me* it absolutely was the wrong thing.

It was the Lord's decision to make, but I stepped in. Even though I realize that many people would not agree with me, I can't think of any reason for ending a life, short of God letting that child die.

SARAH: *to this day I regret it*

**Unless the LORD had given me help, I would soon have
dwelt in the silence of death. (Psalm 94:17)**

I lived a nightmare
first delightful dream
then revolting horror
my roller coaster of emotion
exuberance at the outset
new life, expected birth
then dread of what might be
*   inside me*

some horrible mistake, they said
nature's blunder
malformed misshapen something
a growth within
no telling what defective life
might be hiding there inside
get rid of it, they said
just some faulty tissue
like tonsils or a tumor
do yourself a favor
and have it out

like some cruel brutal nightmare
my fears marched on and on
one panic-ridden step led to another
budding fear blossomed into dread
and no one intervened
no one asked what might have been
no one asked my baby if it wanted
*   life*
no one questioned how I felt about
*   this child*
and no one shouted "stop, wake up"

this slow motion tragedy
plays out still before my very eyes
I watch a horror film inside my head
the plot unwinds in agony

and the starring role is always mine
no hero ever intercedes
no heroine ever intervenes

relentlessly the terrible scenario
unfolds still within my mind
and there's no happy ending
my nightmare always ends in death

quiet now, my child
come out and find your peace
*   within my love*
for I will be your hero
I will interrupt your nightmare
wipe away your tears
cancel all your guilt
blot out your fear and dread
give you life and hope instead

no dream can erase your nightmare
your tragedy is real
my remedy is no fantasy
your pain cannot be healed by
*   fairy tales*

I offer you the love I gave once
*   long ago*
poured out upon my cross
on that dark day
I lived a nightmare of my own
my Father's wrath against your sin
*   unleashed on me*
the Lamb once slain
for you

but now it's over and it's done
it's real—it is no dream
the penalty is paid
the victory has been won
come die my death and live my life

first in baptismal waters
I enfolded you within my arms
and carried you into my grave
to die with me
and out again to share my life
my risen life for you

now again in oral word I place
*   in human mouths to speak*
I pronounce you whole and clean
*   and free from sin*
the holy meal I set before you
is no symbol nor a dream
but reality hid for you
in bread and wine
my body given long ago at Calvary
my blood once shed for you
is yours here in blest reality

so silence now your dread
live no more in bondage
the captive of your fears
the prisoner of your nightmare
come out I say
come out into my truth
and light and peace
the love I give is real and not a dream
in me you're free
so come
and live in me

Lynette

D and C

It's very simple.
        (They're only letters.)
It won't hurt you.
A, B, D, C....................A, B, D, C
        (No, it's wrong -
        It hurts when you're wrong)
A, B, D, C....................Nothing's wrong.
        Wait, I'm sick
        it hurts
        i love you
        i hate you
        no more.....please
D, C..........
        The end.

Lynette wrote this poem a month after her abortion.
She was only 16 years old, in a forced marriage with a man
who beat her. A few months later she wrote another,
inspired by a home economics class bulletin board covered with pictures of babies. It was her last cry for help
before she shut off all her feelings and "formed calluses on
my soul":

Do You Care?
I see those words every time I turn a corner
    and then

Do you care about me?
The hypocrisy of saying yes
    chokes me into silence.
I do, but it's too late
    to tell him that.

Lynette is shedding her calluses now. Her grief and the
years she says she spent running from God have led her to
a calling to help other women who are experiencing the
same pain.

†　†　†　†　†

I was raised in a pretty, little town in Indiana. It's a nice
place to be from but a tough place to grow up, because it
had only 20,000 people and a real small-town attitude.
Unfortunately, it wasn't the best of small-town attitudes. It
was real snippy and gossipy.

I have a sister three and a half years younger. We were
both adopted. My mother has had several types of cancer
and could not have children.

As a child, I always felt that Mom and Dad didn't talk to
each other—literally didn't talk. Not about anything. They
seemed to get along all right, but it seemed like they just
shared the same living space and didn't have any relationship. My father lost his father when he was four years old,
so he really didn't know what it was like to be a father. He
just worked 12 hours a day, six days a week to bring home
the biggest paycheck he could so his family would be
taken care of.

There was always a definite distance. We weren't real
comfortable talking about a lot of things. As I got older,
my mother's primary method of discipline was to put an
open Bible on my place mat and leave the house. I was
supposed to read the passage and feel duly chastised by it

and change my life. She came from a home with a strict, German disciplinarian father. The whole neighborhood lived in fear of him. She was still terrified of him, even when she was in her fifties.

I knew deep down that my parents loved me, but they weren't demonstrative people. I thought of them like I thought of God—as someone who didn't really like us very much, but he had to love us. My parents were the same in my mind.

Religion was important to us. My parents moved to our town for the Christian school; my sister and I both went there. So religion was spoken of, but it wasn't a deep, heartfelt thing. It was more: "This is the thing that should be done, and we are going to do it." I could never seem to make it real to me.

I could never talk to my parents about sex. No. I was in fifth grade when the teachers decided to talk to the girls in the class about the physical changes that we would be going through soon. So they called all the girls and their mothers in one night to see a filmstrip. When we got home that night my mother took me into her bedroom and closed the door. In a very tight, strained voice she said, "Now, I want you to know, here are those things they talked about tonight," and pointed to a box way back on her closet shelf; "but don't ever mention it to your father because he would be terribly embarrassed," and she walked out of the room.

While I was in high school, my parents tried to maintain that same idyllic, "you will always be my baby and under my rule" life. I still had a 10:00 p.m. curfew, even on weekends. My parents seemed to be very suspicious of me. I would come home and find that my room had been ransacked. I was doing only the things they wanted, yet I felt I was being punished for it.

Then my best friend moved away, and I went into a real

depression. I remember wondering why I was going on: my parents didn't trust me; my friend was gone; my girl-friends were all turning into simpering idiots. I left draw-ings of guns and knives all over the house. I cut up my ten-nis shoes with my father's hunting knife as a way to get attention, but my parents didn't react. They didn't care.

At that time, late in my sophomore year, I met an older boy. He was 18 and came from a more lax family and was much more streetwise than I was. I remember hearing that Tom had quite a reputation, and that scared me because I just knew nothing. Oh, I knew the mechanics of sex, but I had no concept of the feelings, emotions, and responsibilities that went with it. We dated over a year before we had sex. I trusted this boy implicitly not to hurt me, but I also felt that I would lose him if I didn't have sex. Later I found out that our first time was his first time too, despite his reputation. We didn't use any birth control, even though I knew that was stupid, but it was too terrify-ing to go out into the world and admit what we were doing. I knew deep down that it was wrong; but I loved him so much and knew we would get married, so I thought that would make it OK retroactively.

I found out the day of my junior prom that I was preg-nant. It was wonderful until I told Tom. I said, "It's positive," and he said, "What do you mean, positive?" I remember the look of shock and terror on his face at a point when I gen-uinely expected him to smile and hug me and be so glad that we could start our lives together like we had talked about. Instead he said, "You are going to get an abortion."

I was like, "What? I don't understand."

He said, "You've got a choice. You can have that kid, or you can have me."

At first I was adamant. I told him that God had given me this child, put it inside my body, and I couldn't do that to it. That was the first time he beat me up. He told me, "You will either go and have this done, or I will beat it out of you. I am not raising this child."

I remember that night spending hours in prayer, telling God that I didn't know what to do. This boy was my life; I was totally committed to him. I prayed to God, "Please God, take this child. Take him back and take care of him until the time when I can have a child. I can't now." I was sure that God was ready to take the baby's soul back into heaven.

I was such a romantic. I had bought it all, hook, line, and sinker, the whole Ali McGraw-Ryan O'Neal type thing. It was going to be melodramatic and painful, but wonderful so long as we had each other. I trusted in that. I had no reason not to. I didn't know how hateful and lying people could be, because I had always been protected from that. I just didn't know what else to do.

The next day I went to Tom and said, "Fine. You'll have what you want."

Through the course of this relationship, I had alienated myself from my parents. I would have done anything for Tom, and they knew it. They hated him. When they found out we were sleeping together, they hated him even more.

I had severe morning sickness and started showing right away, so there wasn't any way I could hide it from them. My father's only comment was, "You two *will* get married. Tomorrow we'll all go down to the courthouse." I was underage so they had to sign for me. The next day they took us to court and signed the papers. When the judge handed us our marriage license, my mother had such hysterics my father had to take her out.

We stood outside the courthouse and I asked Tom, "What do you want to do?"

"I don't know, what do you want to do?" Tom answered.

"Why wait? Let's just go upstairs and get married."

So we did. We didn't have a ring; we didn't have a witness—the judge called in a secretary. When it was over, I went to work at my summer job.

That afternoon, at four o'clock, I had an appointment with the doctor to begin the abortion procedure. Since I was 14 weeks along, I had to be dilated first. My parents didn't know. There was no way I could have brought this to them. I hadn't even told them that we'd gotten married that morning.

I stayed with Tom that night, and the next morning we got up and went for the rest of the procedure. I was convinced that the Lord had accepted the soul of my child back and that everything was going to be all right.

They hadn't told me how much it was going to hurt. They didn't tell me about how unsettling the noise is and how bright the lights are. I remember, during the procedure itself, that I was sort of praying. Yes, I guess it was praying; but at the same time I was telling myself, "Don't think. Whatever you do, don't think about what they are doing."

Afterward I think I passed out. I slept for a couple of hours. They told me all the usual things—about the bleeding and to call a doctor if you get a fever. We went out and bought our wedding rings.

I moved in with Tom's family. They already had Tom's grandparents living with them, so we were three generations in one tiny house.

Several weeks later my mother was throwing around some pointed questions about the baby. She would never have come right out and asked. I said, "There is no baby. I told you before that Tom hits me," and I walked away.

By nine months into my marriage, still a senior in high school, I had already gone through four beatings. My girl-friends had no idea what I was going through, and they stayed away from me. My parents really didn't want much to do with me. Some teachers saw my bruises and asked me about them, but I told them I'd been in an accident or other excuses.

I went to my pastor for counseling, but he didn't keep it to himself. Other people in the church found out about the abortion, and it quickly spread through school. Then my parents found out. They wanted to know why I hadn't told them. My only thought was, "I can't talk to you about what clothes to buy. How could I talk to you about the crisis my life has become?" I had two black eyes the day they talked to me, but they didn't ask about that.

I started thinking about the abortion. My locker was right across from the home-ec room, and there was a bulletin board about child care, with pictures of babies. As I looked at that, I thought about my child, the child I had such great dreams for. I was sure it was a boy and was going to name him David. Before the abortion, I would talk to him and write letters to him. I was so in love with him; but thinking about it was more than I could handle, so I just put it aside. I got pretty hard, pretty quick. I got a lot of calluses on my soul; I couldn't feel anything.

Tom and I separated in the spring. I moved back home, but it was hard. My parents tried to pretend that none of it happened, that I was still their innocent sixteen-year-old. After a month I went back to him. I still felt a strong sense of commitment. I kept thinking that I had promised to love him for better or for worse.

We bought a mobile home, so we were finally on our own. It was wonderful at first, but it didn't last. A few weeks later I was talking on the phone to a girlfriend, and he asked for something. I said, "In just a minute," and he raised his hand to hit me.

I had had enough. "Go ahead, hit me," I shouted. "Can you hear me, Katie? He's going to hit me. If we lose the connection, call the police." He was so furious he just walked out.

I moved in with a series of friends then, so he couldn't

find me. I called my parents, but I wouldn't tell them where I was. I kept going to school just like a normal high school student.

I got the marriage annulled. The next week I graduated from high school. Strangely enough, after that we were fairly civil to each other.

I lived at home for the summer and continued to work as a waitress. My parents didn't trust me. They searched my room regularly; they opened my mail; they followed me on dates. We had a lot of shouting matches about it.

Then in the fall, I went off to college. Before I left, my mother said, "I never had this opportunity. I hope you take advantage of it and don't screw it up like you do everything else." So I was determined to succeed. And I did.

While I was there, several girls became pregnant and came to me for advice. No one knew about my abortion. When the subject came up, I would just shrug and say, "It's been done. You'll survive."

I had walked out of my church when my confidence was betrayed, and I never went back. I didn't trust anyone at that point, but at college I made some close friends. Those young women showed me what unconditional acceptance and friendship were.

I dated a young man, his name was Gary, all through college; and everyone expected that we would get married. He knew about my first marriage and the abortion. During my junior year, I was raped. Gary drove all night to be with me and proposed on the spot. I said yes.

Two months before the wedding I had some reservations and wanted to get out of it. But my mother said, "It's all paid for, and you are going through with it."

So I did. We were married, and after I graduated, we moved to the East Coast. This man didn't beat me, but he had his own problems. He was very cold and withdrawn, and he was verbally abusive. He liked to humiliate me in front of our friends.

I became pregnant once during that marriage, but it was a tubal pregnancy. The doctor said it could have been caused by scar tissue from the previous abortion. I lost the tube and one ovary.

The second marriage lasted for three years and dragged out in court for another two before we were finally divorced.

During those years, I continued to push down any thoughts of the abortion. After my divorce, I concentrated on my career. I was the first woman in my industry, the first women in sales. I was going to set fire to the world. I tried to be so busy that no one could touch me or hurt me again.

But eventually I met another man and began to open myself emotionally again. That relationship didn't work out, but during the time I was responding to some warmth in my life I began to feel inside the tug to return to my faith. I became involved with a Christian mission, and, through it, I met some wonderful Christian friends as well as a pastor who helped me a lot.

He is the person who helped me to finally deal with the abortion. For years I had asked God to forgive me. I knew in my head that he had, but I never let go of it. I continued to punish myself for it.

When I told this young pastor the story of the abortion, he reached over and patted the top of my head. Then he read to me from the Psalms, the passage about the soul groaning and falling upon the couch weeping, but how the Lord will not despise a contrite heart. There was such forgiveness and such comfort in what he read. Then he gave me a blessing and a big hug that lasted as long as my tears did. From that moment, it's really been over. I could finally begin to talk about it and deal with it, because it's over. It was never over before.

Now I can see how much that abortion changed my outlook. I couldn't afford to look at God's law, because the law hurt. I couldn't accept the gospel, because I wasn't worthy of it. I didn't know how to come to forgiveness. I just didn't understand how much Christ can truly forgive.

I surely didn't know the freedom of being forgiven. People talk about a weight being lifted off. Well, it's real. Since then I've been able to go back and forgive the people who have hurt me, and to rebuild relationships. I'm finally building a relationship with my parents. And I'm starting to become close to my sister—for years my parents wouldn't let her talk to me. A few weeks ago, I was the maid of honor at her wedding.

Now I'm single, living alone. I'm putting a lot of time into the mission church. My faith is so much more of a heartfelt thing than it ever was before. I'm learning how to trust again. All through my life everyone I trusted hurt me, so I just stopped. But now it's coming back.

For me the abortion is over. I'm very sorry that it happened. It's not a pretty part of my past, but it is in my past. I'm not proud of the fact that I spent so long running away from God, but I'm so thankful that in his patience and his obstinacy and his faithfulness to his promise to take care of his children, that he kept trying to pull me closer to him. My self-esteem is much higher now because I'm starting to see myself the way he sees me.

I've decided to go back to school for a master's degree in counseling, and I plan to work with women who have had abortions. I'm interviewing with several schools right now. I have to admit I'm a little frightened, but I'm also eager to get started. I feel very strongly that the Lord will bless whatever he sets my hand to. I'm really starting to understand what it means when the Bible says that the Lord does all things for good.

LYNETTE: *I got a lot of calluses on my soul*

**I am worn out from groaning; all night long I flood my bed
with weeping and drench my couch with tears.** (Psalm 6:6)

*damaged skin defends itself
the calluses grow thick
the skin's own shield from further
   harm*

*a damaged heart defends itself as well
a callus forms within the soul
to shield the heart from deeper pain*

*but a callus has no life within
a screen of death to mask out pain
and when you live behind that
   screen
you feel no pain
because you feel no more
something dies deep down inside
you're safe
but dead within*

*the messages I got were mixed
as mixed up as my heart
come to me, they said—I hate you
go away, they said—I love you*

*those who hated hurt me a lot
but those who said they loved me
hurt the most
I didn't know what love was all
   about
love hurts a lot was all I knew
the bruises on my body
the bruises on my soul
my battered self cried out for love
but found more pain
the pain of unborn infant life
   snuffed out*

*and something else died deep inside
besides that child
all my dreams lay shattered on the
   floor
the broken pieces of my life
engulfed in pain and hurt*

*my trust betrayed
I hid from love
because it hurt too much
withdrawn inside a calloused soul
I felt no pain
I was safe within
but dead*

*listen carefully my child
my words breathe life for you
my love, which is your life*

*no need to hide from me
this love of mine
is safe to trust
for greater love has no man than this
that he lay down his life
for those who are his friends*

*and this great love is yours in me
you are my friend
for whom I shed my blood
I gave my life in death
to rescue you from harm*

*that day at Calvary I was your sin
I cried your tears and bore your pain
including all the guilt you wore*